Essential Histories

The Greek and Persian Wars 499–386 BC

Essential Histories

The Greek and Persian Wars 499–386 BC

Philip de Souza

Routledge
Taylor & Francis Group
NEW YORK AND LONDON

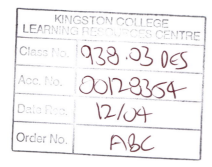
This hardback edition is published by Routledge, an imprint
of the Taylor & Francis Group, by arrangement with
Osprey Publishing Ltd., Oxford, England.

For information, please address the publisher:
Routledge (USA)
29 West 35th Street, New York, NY 10001
www.routledge-ny.com

Routledge (UK)
11 New Fetter Lane, London EC4P 4EE
www.routledge.co.uk

First published 2002 under the title Essential Histories 36:
The Greek and Persian Wars 499–386 BC by Osprey Publishing Ltd.,
Elms Court, Chapel Way, Botley, Oxford OX2 9LP
© 2003 Osprey Publishing Ltd.

ISBN 0-415-96854-2

Printed and bound in China on acid-free paper

03 04 05 06 07   10 9 8 7 6 5 4 3 2 1

Library of Congress Cataloging-in-Publication Data

De Souza, Philip.
  The Greek and Persian Wars, 499-386 B.C. / Philip de Souza.
      p. cm. -- (Essential Histories)
Originally published: Oxford: Osprey Publishing Ltd., 2002.
Includes bibliographical references and index.
  ISBN 0-415-96854-2
  1. Greece--History--Persian Wars, 500-449 B.C. 2.
Greece--History--Spartan and Theban Supremacies, 404-362
B.C. I. Title.
II. Series.
  DF225.D44 2003
  938'.03--dc21
                                    2003009684

Contents

Introduction

Herodotus and the invention of history

Part of the fascination of the Greek and Persian Wars lies in the fact that they had a great influence on the history of the western world. By preventing the Persians from conquering Greece, the Athenians, the Spartans and other Greeks made it possible for their own unique and highly influential culture to develop independently of Persian dominance. Equally important, however, is the fact that the events of the Persian Wars are recounted in one of the most important and influential works of Classical Greek literature, *The Histories* of Herodotus. Herodotus was born in the first half of the fifth century BC, in the Greek city of Halikarnassos, which was on the edge of the Persian Empire. He travelled extensively, collecting information from people about themselves and their ancestors. He was able to talk to many who had experienced the events themselves, or who had heard first-hand accounts from others who were involved. The Persian Wars are, therefore, the first wars for which there exists a detailed historical narrative written by someone who was able to obtain detailed and reliable information. Herodotus' account can to some extent be supplemented by some other sources, including later Greek and Latin writers and the official documents of Athens and Persia, but he is the most significant source.

The idea of recording great achievements for posterity was not in itself a new one. Egyptian, Babylonian and Assyrian rulers had long been accustomed to setting up memorials to their own greatness, inscribing them with official versions of events. What makes Herodotus' work so special is that he sought to go beyond the mere collection of these records and to enquire into their origins and causes. He was consciously looking for explanations of the events. In this respect Herodotus can be seen as part of a much wider intellectual and cultural tradition of philosophical and scientific speculation and enquiry. There is also an element of learning from the events. Herodotus offers his readers his investigations into the origins and causes of the events he narrates, as well as his interpretations of their wider significance. He invites his readers to learn from his *Histories*, although some of his lessons can seem strange to a modern audience. This is how he introduces his account:

These are the enquiries (the Greek word is 'histories') *of Herodotus of Halikarnassos, which he sets down so that he can preserve the memory of what these men have done, and ensure that the wondrous achievements of the Greeks and Persians* (he uses the Greek word *barbaroi*, meaning foreigners) *do not lose their deserved fame, and also to record why they went to war with each other.*

Chronology

AUTHOR'S NOTE ON DATES: All dates are BC. The official Athenian year, which was often used by Greek historians as a dating device, began and ended in midsummer. As a result some of the dates in this book are given in the form 478/77, which indicates the Athenian year that began in the summer of 478 and ended in the summer of 477.

The coming of the Persians

The enquiries of the Greek historian Herodotus into the wars between the Greeks and the Persians led him to conclude that their origins lay in the rise to power of the Persian Empire under the first of the Achaemenid kings, Kyros the Great. It was Kyros who conquered the kingdom of Lydia in 547. The king of Lydia, Kroisos, had tried to take advantage of the turmoil caused by Kyros' seizure of the Median Empire by invading its western territories. Kyros met the Lydian king in battle in Kappadokia and forced him to withdraw. Kroisos stood his army down, thinking that there would be no further fighting, but Kyros pressed on to Sardis, the Lydian capital and laid siege to the city, which he captured after only two weeks. Kroisos had brought the prosperous Greek cities of Ionia on the western coast of Asia Minor under his rule and made them pay tribute to him. After his defeat they acknowledged the rule of Kyros, but many of them participated in a revolt of the Lydians and had to be brought back under Persian control by force. Some of the Greeks chose to flee overseas rather than submit to the Persians. Half the people of Phokaia emigrated to the western Mediterranean, where many Greek cities were already flourishing, and most of the inhabitants of Teos founded a new city at Abdera on the Thracian coast. The larger islands off the coast of Ionia retained their independence for some time, but by 518 the Persians controlled all of Asia Minor and most of the eastern Aegean islands, including Lesbos, Chios and Samos. In keeping with their practice elsewhere in the territories under their control the Persian kings installed or sponsored local aristocrats as rulers of the Greek cities of Asia Minor and the nearby islands. These men were called 'tyrants', a Lydian word used by the Greeks to describe an individual ruler who was not necessarily an hereditary monarch, but who had not been elected or put in power by overwhelming popular support. These local rulers were answerable to a Persian governor, called a 'satrap' – an Old Persian word meaning 'guardian of the land' – who normally resided in Sardis. The Persians also exacted tribute from the Ionians, probably at the same level as the Lydian kings before them.

The Ionian revolt

In 499 the Persians launched a major naval expedition against Naxos, the largest and most prosperous of the Cycladic islands. Herodotus presents this expedition as the result of an appeal by some exiled Naxian aristocrats to Aristagoras, the ruling tyrant of Miletos, to help them force their compatriots to accept them back and return them to power. Miletos was one of the largest and most important Ionian cities. It had enjoyed privileged, semi-independent status in relation to the Lydian kings, which the Persians allowed to continue. According to Herodotus' account Aristagoras said that he did not have sufficient resources to attack Naxos, but he persuaded Artaphernes, the Persian satrap of Lydia, to help. Artaphernes then obtained King Dareios' consent to assemble a fleet of 200 ships and a substantial Persian army to invade Naxos. It is unlikely that such a large force would have been authorised by the king unless he expected to conquer the island, paving the way for further Persian expansion across the Aegean. From Naxos it is only a short sail to the islands of Paros and Andros and thence

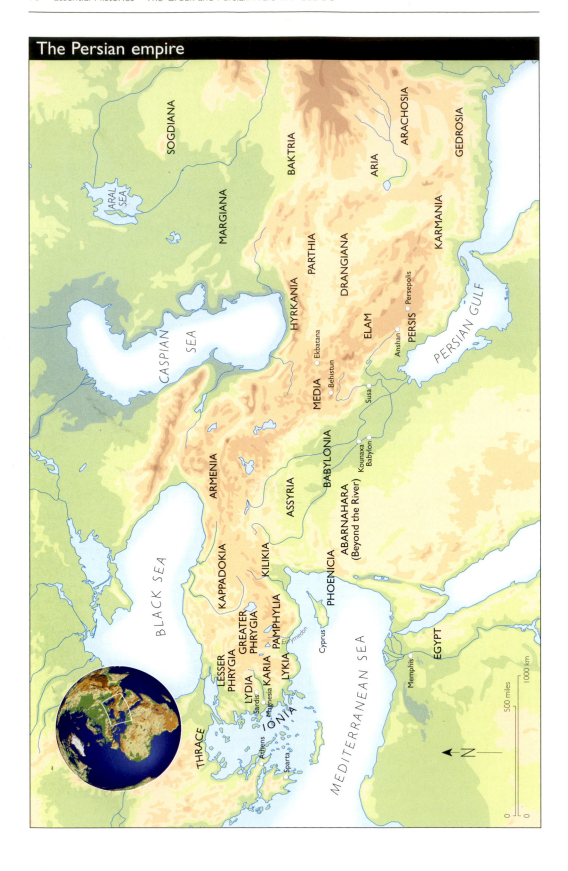

The Persian empire

SOGDIANA

BAKTRIA

ARACHOSIA

GEDROSIA

ARIA

ARAL
SEA

MARGIANA

KARMANIA

PARTHIA

DRANGIANA

HYRKANIA

ELAM

• Persepolis

PERSIS

Anshan •

CASPIAN
SEA

MEDIA   • Ekbatana

• Behistun

Susa •

PERSIAN GULF

ARMENIA

ASSYRIA

BABYLONIA

Kounaxa •
Babylon •

ABARNAHARA
(Beyond the River')

BLACK SEA

KAPPADOKIA

KILIKIA

PHOENICIA

LESSER
PHRYGIA

GREATER
PHRYGIA

PAMPHYLIA

△ Eurymedon

Cyprus •

MEDITERRANEAN SEA

EGYPT

LYDIA

KARIA

LYKIA

Memphis •

Sardis •

Magnesia •

IONIA

THRACE

Athens •

Sparta •

500 miles

1000 km

N

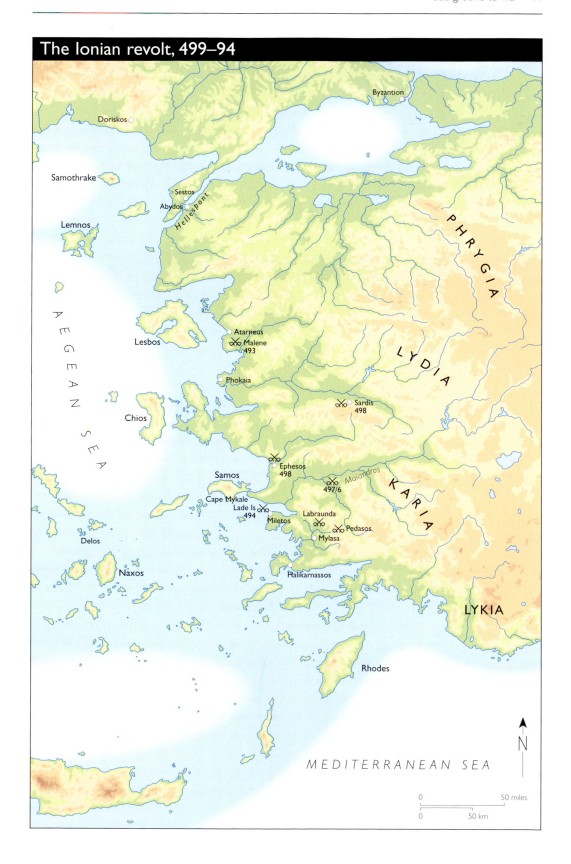

The Ionian revolt, 499–94

Byzantion

Doriskos

Samothrake

Sestos
Abydos
Hellespont

Lemnos

PHRYGIA

A E G E A N   S E A

Lesbos

Atarneus
Malene
493

Phokaia

LYDIA

Sardis
498

Chios

Ephesos
498

Samos

497/6

Maiandros

Cape Mykale
Lade Is
494
Miletos

Labraunda

KARIA

Pedasos
Mylasa

Delos

Halikarnassos

Naxos

LYKIA

Rhodes

N

M E D I T E R R A N E A N   S E A

0   50 miles

0   50 km

to Euboia and the mainland of Greece. It seems probable, therefore, that the initiative for the whole expedition came from the Persians, and that the exiled Naxian aristocrats' appeal to Aristagoras provided a pretext for the attack. Aristagoras also seems to have undertaken to pay a major part of the costs of the expedition, possibly on the understanding that he could recoup his outlay from the plunder of Naxos. The manpower for the fleet of 200 trireme warships was mostly drawn from the Greek cities of Asia Minor, but the army included a substantial contingent of Persian troops and was under the command of Megabates, a cousin of the Great King. When the invasion force arrived at Naxos, however, the inhabitants were ready for them. They had probably heard of the extensive preparations, particularly the assembly of the fleet, from maritime traders who sailed between the Cyclades and the mainland. They gathered their population and a stock of supplies into the main city of Naxos, which had strong defensive walls, and withstood a siege of four months. After their own supplies had been exhausted the Persians gave up and their forces returned to the city of Myous on the mainland.

At this point Aristagoras decided to precipitate a full-scale revolt of the Ionian Greeks against the Persians. His own motivations are difficult to determine. He seems to have quarrelled with Megabates, the Persian commander, although the trivial reason for their falling out given by Herodotus, namely that Megabates had mistreated an Ionian naval captain called Skylax, is unlikely to be the whole truth. Aristagoras had underwritten the cost of the failed expedition and now he, or rather the city of Miletos, could not afford to pay up. It also seems that his own city of Miletos was, like many other Greek cities at this time, becoming a hotbed of political discontent. The Persian-sponsored tyrants were unpopular with the majority of the citizens, who wanted a far greater say in the way their cities were governed. Aristagoras decided to offer himself as the leader of a revolutionary reforming movement in Ionia that would throw off the burden of Persian rule, remove the tyrants and install governments based on the principal of *isonomia* (equal rights) for all citizens. Aristagoras declared that he was giving up his position as tyrant of Miletos, although he continued to be the dominant political figure there. The tyrants of the main Ionian cities and islands, including Erythrai, Teos, Samos, and Chios, were rounded up and expelled. Most of them went to Sardis, where they joined the entourage of the satrap Artaphernes in the hope that they would be reinstated by their Persian patrons. The newly liberated Ionian citizens proceeded to elect their own generals for the imminent military confrontation with the Persians.

The enthusiasm with which the Ionians responded to Aristagoras' call for a revolt was partly due to the autocratic nature of Persian rule. That is not to say that the tyrants or the Persian satraps who appointed them were excessively harsh in the way that they governed the Greeks, but the Ionians clearly resented having to obey tyrants who were appointed from among their fellow countrymen at the whim of a king whose court was far away and whose priorities rarely coincided with their own. Some of the Ionian cities and islands had been developing a form of democratic government when they came under Persian influence. Such developments continued in mainland Greece, especially in Athens, but the move to widespread popular participation in government was prematurely halted in Ionia. King Dareios, whom the Greeks referred to as 'the tradesman', demanded manpower for military expeditions and money, in the form of a regular tribute, paid in silver at a higher level than previously. The campaigns were against people like the Skythians, whom the Greeks could not possibly see as a threat to their own lands, and the silver was hoarded in distant Persia, or spent on gifts and wages for other foreigners. The Ionians got little in return for their annexation by the Persians. Archaeological studies have indicated that their share in the maritime trade of the

Mediterranean was declining towards the end of the sixth century. They may have felt that the cities of mainland Greece, Italy and Sicily, as well as the Phoenicians were doing well at their expense, and that they needed to be free of Persian control in order to recover their economic prosperity.

The Ionians were not so foolish as to believe that they could throw off the yoke of Persian rule unaided and they immediately sought assistance from their kinsmen in mainland Greece. Aristagoras travelled to Sparta to ask the strongest of the Greek states for aid, but he was unsuccessful. The Spartans were too preoccupied with their own problems, including a long-standing rivalry with the city of Argos, to send an army overseas. The Argives had recently received a dire oracular warning from the sanctuary of the god Apollo in Delphi which prophesied their own impending doom along with that of Miletos, so they were unwilling to help. It is probable that Aristagoras approached several other leading Greek states with similar results, but he did manage to persuade Athens and the Euboian city of Eretria to send some warships.

Why did the Athenians and Eretrians agree to help the Ionians, when the Spartans and others refused? A greater feeling of kinship with the Ionians may have been one reason. They spoke more or less the same dialect of Greek, their religious festivals were very similar, and they believed that they shared a common ancestry. Athens was thought to be the place from which the Greeks who settled in Ionia had first sailed across the Aegean. They had also had close diplomatic and economic ties before the coming of the Persians and they now had a common interest in democratic government. The Athenians had previously made an alliance with the Persian satrap Artaphernes, seeking to obtain his backing in their disputes with other Greek states, but they no longer respected this treaty because the Persians were sheltering Hippias, the former tyrant of Athens, at Sigeion. Hippias entertained hopes of being restored to power in Athens with Persian assistance. Aristagoras painted a

Oracles

Oracles were taken very seriously by the Greeks, especially those that were issued by the priestess of Apollo at Delphi, although they were not always given in terms which were easy to understand. The historian Herodotus quotes several Delphic oracles which he says were later seen to have been accurate prophesies concerning the triumphs and failures of the Greeks and the Persians.

The oracle concerning Miletos was as follows:

Then shall you, Miletos, the contriver of many evil deeds,
Yourself become a banquet and a splendid prize for many,
Your wives shall bathe the feet of many long-haired men;
And my temple at Didyma will be cared for by others.

It is clear that the oracle is a warning of impending doom for Miletos. The description of Miletos as 'the contriver of many evil deeds' indicates that there was a widespread prejudice among the people of mainland Greece against this rich and powerful city. Herodotus explains that this prophecy referred to the capture and sack of Miletos by the Persians, who wore their hair and beards long. They killed most of the men and enslaved the women and children. Didyma was a sanctuary of Apollo in Milesian territory, which also housed an oracle. It was plundered and burnt by the Persians.

picture for the assembly of Athenian citizens of the Persians as militarily weak and ripe for plundering by a combined Greek force. The Athenians voted to send a military expedition in 20 ships under the command of Melanthios to aid the Ionians against the Persians. Herodotus, looking ahead to the

ABOVE A fifth-century Athenian tetradachm, a silver coin of high value. The Athenians had a good supply of silver which they mined intensively during the fifth and fourth centuries. They also gained a great deal of silver coinage from their subject allies, who paid tribute to the Athenians at a similar rate to that which many of them had paid it to the Persians before 478. (Ancient Art and Architecture)

RIGHT A gold plaque from a large fourth-century treasure hoard found near the Oxus river in the north-eastern region of the Persian Empire. The figure is of a priest in the typical dress of the Medes, comprising a belted tunic, trousers and boots. He wears a soft cap that has flaps to cover the ears and chin to protect them from the wind. Persian and Median religious rituals emphasised the power of natural phenomena like fire, water and the fertile earth. (Ancient Art and Architecture)

battles of Marathon, Thermopylai, Salamis and Plataia, comments that these ships were the origin of troubles for both Greeks and Persians. By encouraging and assisting the rebels, the Athenians, and the Eretrians, who sent five warships to help in the revolt, might have hoped to dissuade the Persians from further expansion westwards. They must have been keenly aware of how vulnerable they were to attack if a Persian conquest of the Cyclades were achieved.

In 498 the Athenian and Eretrian contingents joined a mainly Milesian army at Ephesos. From there the combined force marched inland to attack the Persian provincial capital at Sardis. They took the satrap Artaphernes by surprise. He abandoned the lower part of the city and took refuge in the citadel. He held off the Ionians and their allies and waited for reinforcements to arrive. Even the accidental burning of much of the

This bronze hoplite's helmet of the Corinthian type is inscribed with the name Dendas, perhaps the person who dedicated it in a sanctuary around the year 500. Such helmets afforded good protection to the wearer, but they severely restricted vision and hearing, causing the hoplites' reliance on the coherence of their formation. (Ancient Art and Architecture)

city, including the temple of Cybele, the Great Mother Goddess, did not break the resolve of Artaphernes and his Lydian and Persian troops. When a strong Persian cavalry force approached, the attackers withdrew but they were overtaken near Ephesos and heavily defeated. Aristagoras' prediction of easy pickings had proved to be wrong. The Athenians and Eretrians embarked on their ships and returned home with stories of the Persians' determination and the superiority of their cavalry. The Ionians were left to face the wrath of the Persian king on their own.

The Ionians decided to take the initiative once more by sending ships north and south to the Hellespont and Karia, to encourage wider rebellion among King Dareios' subjects. They also supported a revolt among the Greek cities of Cyprus, but this was short-lived. In 497 a large Persian army was despatched to Cyprus on a fleet drawn from the cities of Phoenicia. The tyrants whom the Persians had established as rulers in the cities of Salamis and Kourion deserted to the Persian side at a vital moment and, in spite of naval assistance from the Ionians, the Cypriots were defeated.

Also in 497 Dareios sent more Persian armies to regain control of the Hellespontine region and Karia, but one of them, under the command of his son-in-law Daurises, was ambushed by the Karians at Pedasos and almost completely destroyed. Although his other commanders enjoyed more success to the north, this defeat was such a major setback that Dareios had to wait until 494 to launch a strong land and sea offensive against the main seat of the revolt, Miletos. By this time, Aristagoras had been driven out of Miletos by his political rivals and killed. The loss of their main leader was to have a serious affect on the cohesion of the revolt, and distrust of those who tried to take his place hampered the co-ordination of the fight against the Persians. When Histiaios, the father-in-law and predecessor of Aristagoras as tyrant of Miletos returned to his city, ostensibly on a peace mission from Dareios, but actually to offer himself as the new leader of the revolt, he was driven off by the Milesians and had to take refuge in Mytilene on the island of Lesbos.

The nearest thing the Ionians had to a common political organisation was their *koinon*, a religious assembly which met annually at the Panionion, a sanctuary of Poseidon in the territory of Priene. This assembly was not meant to be a political one and it lacked the structures to produce a unified leadership. When they finally did manage to gather their naval forces at the island of Lade, off the coast of Miletos, there was a dispute over who should take command. The naval forces at the battle of Lade show the relative size, prosperity and power of the Ionians. There were 80 ships from Miletos, 12 from Priene, three from Myous, 17 from Teos, eight from Erythrai and three from Phokaia. The main islands furnished some of the largest contingents, 100 from Chios, 60 from Samos and 70 from the island of Lesbos, whose cities were not formally members of the Ionian League, but who nevertheless participated in the revolt. Eventually Dionysios of Phokaia, who led the smallest contingent, was put in charge, but although his appointment prevented arguments among the larger states, he lacked the authority to hold the different contingents together. In any case the combined Ionian fleet of 353 ships was only a little more than half the size of the Persian naval force of 600, which included ships from Egypt and Kilikia, but was mainly provided by the Phoenician cities. First the Samians deserted the cause, with the exception of 11 brave, but foolhardy, captains. Next the Lesbians followed suit and fled for their island homes. Without a major naval force to protect it Miletos was vulnerable to assault. The Persian commanders brought in expert military engineers from Phoenicia who forced their way into the city with the help of mines and battering rams. The rest of the cities and islands were gradually reduced to submission and punished for their revolt. Herodotus tells a grim tale of cities and their principal sanctuaries being burnt down, men killed, girls taken off to harems, with castrated boys as their eunuch attendants, while the remaining women and children were sold as slaves.

There were eventually some positive outcomes of the revolt for the Ionian Greeks. In 493 the satrap Artaphernes required representatives of the Greek states to come to Sardis and swear oaths that they would submit all inter-city disputes to arbitration. This implies that their individual governments were functioning well enough for envoys to be selected; the arbitrators were probably chosen by the Ionian *koinon*. Artaphernes also reassessed the amounts of annual tribute that each city and island had to pay to the king, making this burden more acceptable and less likely to provoke rebellion in the future. The following year King Dareios sent another son-in-law, Mardonios, to take charge of the region. He removed the remaining tyrants and allowed the Greeks under his control to establish democratic governments, according to the principal of *isonomia* which had been one

This fifth-century Athenian red-figure painted cup by the artist Epiktetos shows an archer wearing the typical tunic, trousers and hood of Iranian mercenary units in the Persian armies that invaded Greece. Although the Greeks did use archers and other missile troops in warfare, they did not form a substantial proportion of their armies, whereas the Persians and other Near-Eastern peoples often relied heavily on them in battle. (Ashmolean)

of the rallying cries of the revolt. Mardonios' appointment had another purpose, however: to begin the next stage of the Persian advance into the Aegean. He took his fleet and army across the Hellespont into Thrace and he received the surrender of the island of Thasos, along with its fleet of triremes. From there he moved along the northern coastline of the Aegean towards Macedon. A fierce storm claimed 300 ships off the promontory of Mount Athos, but Mardonios had prepared the way for a possible invasion of the Greek mainland.

Persia, Sparta and Athens

Kyros the Great and the Persian Empire

The Persians were part of a group of ancient peoples who spoke languages similar to modern Iranian. They probably originated in central Asia as nomadic cattle-herders, but by the end of the tenth century they had settled in the region known as Persia (modern Fars), on the south-eastern end of the Zagros mountains. Assyrian documents from the ninth century onwards mention them alongside the Medes, who occupied an area to the north and west. The powerful kingdom of Elam had controlled Persia until the mid-seventh century, but after Elamite power was weakened by the Assyrian king, Ashurbanipal, in 646 the Persians seem to have become increasingly autonomous, developing a small state of their own under the rule of a royal family whose seat of power was the Elamite city of Anshan. The fourth ruler of this fledgling kingdom, Kyros II, known as 'Kyros the Great', came to the throne in 559. His kingdom was attacked in 550 by the Median king, Astyages. Kyros persuaded Astyages' army to rebel against their king and they handed him over to Kyros as a prisoner. Kyros then marched into the Median city of Ekbatana and was recognised as the new ruler of the Medes. During the next 20 years Kyros used the combined strength of the Persians and the Medes to conquer Lydia, Assyria and Babylonia and increased his empire to the east by bringing Baktria and Sogdiana under his control. In 530 he was killed fighting to subdue a revolt among some of the Baktrian tribes and his son Kambyses succeeded him.

Kambyses directed his main efforts towards the conquest of Egypt. The Egyptian pharaoh, Amasis, had created a powerful navy and sought alliances with several states in the Mediterranean region, including the Greeks of Sparta and Samos, in an effort to resist the Persian advance. Kambyses had to create his own navy, manned by his maritime subjects in Ionia, Phoenicia and Kilikia. He launched his assault on Egypt in 525 and captured the new pharaoh, Psammetikos, after a 10-day siege at Memphis. He spent the next three years consolidating his control of Egypt.

In 522 Kambyses was on his way back to Persia when he fell from his horse and died. The circumstances of his death are mysterious and there is a suggestion that it was not an accident. He did not have a son, so he should have been succeeded by his brother, Bardiya, but an ambitious aristocrat called Dareios led a palace coup which resulted in the assassination of Bardiya and the installation of Dareios, a distant relative of the royal family, as the new king. These dramatic events plunged the Persian Empire into chaos and civil war which lasted for over a year. Dareios was able to count on the support of several leading Persians whose armies remained loyal to him in spite of his unorthodox seizure of power. Eventually he subdued all the rival aristocrats and several local dynasts who seized on the internal unrest as an opportunity to throw off the yoke of Persian rule. Dareios inaugurated a new Persian dynasty, known as the Achaemenids, because they traced their line back to the Persian Achaemenes, an ancestor of Kyros the Great. Dareios added parts of central Asia and most of north-west India to the Persian Empire, he campaigned unsuccessfully against the Skythians of the western Black Sea region and he extended the territory under his rule into Europe by conquering the parts of Thrace which lay along the northern coastline of the Aegean.

Dareios the Great King

The Persian king Dareios was a usurper who came to the throne as the result of a coup and the assassination of the rightful king. Nevertheless, in his official version of events, inscribed on a high rockface at Behistun in northern Iran, beside the royal road from Ekbatana to Babylon, he proclaimed that he was the legitimate successor of Kambyses and that his kingship was sanctified by Ahuramazda, the patron god of the Achaemenid rulers. The following extracts from the inscription show how Dareios wanted to be thought of and how he regarded the empire over which he ruled.

I am Dareios the Great King, the king of kings, the King of Persia, the king of all lands … So says Dareios the King: Eight times were my family kings and I am the ninth king in succession from my family. So says Dareios the King: I am king by the grace of Ahuramazda. Ahuramazda gave me the kingship. The following lands belong to me. I am their king by the grace of Ahuramazda: Persia, Elam, Babylonia, Assyria, Arabia, Egypt, the Peoples on the Sea (Phoenicia), Lydia, Ionia, Media, Armenia, Kappadokia, Parthia, Drangiana, Aria, Arachosia and Makan, 23 lands in all … So says Dareios the king: In these lands anyone who was loyal I treated well, anyone who was faithless I punished severely. By the grace of Ahuramazda these lands obeyed my rule. Whatever I told them to do, was done …

The inscription was written in three languages, Elamite, the *lingua franca* of much of the empire, Akkadian, the language of the kings of Babylon, and Old High Persian, the official language of the Persian kings. Because this language had never been written before, a new cuneiform script had to be devised for it.

Although the Persian king was known officially as the 'Great King, the king of kings, the king of all lands', his power was not absolute. In practice he relied on the support and co-operation of a large Persian aristocracy whom he was obliged to provide with positions of wealth and power in the newly conquered lands. Hence these lands were divided into provinces and each province was administered by a Persian aristocrat, a satrap. One way to explain the dramatic rise of the Persian Empire is in terms of the ambitions of its aristocracy. The need to satisfy the ambitions of these men was a major reason why Kyros and his successors embarked on campaigns of imperial expansion.

Persian nobles had a long tradition of being fierce warriors and independent aristocrats, so they did not accept a minor role in the hierarchy of the empire. Individuals who were closely related to the king were often made the satraps of large or strategically important provinces, while others were given command over armies or other positions of responsibility. They lived in magnificent palaces and enjoyed the use of large estates in the provinces. The public distribution of prestigious gifts, particularly items of gold and silver, was a method used by the kings to indicate who were the most favoured nobles. The Persians maintained their cohesion and distinctiveness in several ways, including their dress, their use of the Persian language and the education of their sons. Persian boys spent the first five years of their lives away from their fathers in the company of their mothers and other women of the household, but thereafter were taught to be soldiers and rulers. It was said that the Persians expected three things above all from their sons, that they should ride a horse, use a bow and speak the truth.

The ruling Persian élite did not remain completely apart from the subject peoples of the empire. Intermarriage between Persians and non-Persians was encouraged, with the daughters of Persian nobles marrying local princes and the Persians taking local aristocratic women as wives or concubines.

Kyros had adopted a policy of respecting local traditions and retaining some local aristocrats and religious leaders in his administration of Media, Lydia and Babylonia, and Kambyses and Dareios followed this policy in Egypt and elsewhere. People from conquered lands who had been in positions of power were often granted high status and were accepted into the king's court with the honorary title of 'royal friend'. Similar treatment was sometimes granted to exiles from states outside the empire who sought the protection and assistance of the Great King.

A golden dagger with a pommel in the form of two lion heads. It was probably made in the fifth century as a present for someone in the court of the Persian king. Such gifts from the king to his nobles both symbolised that the recipient enjoyed royal favour and transferred some of the enormous wealth of the Achaemenid kings to their Persian aristocrats. (Ancient Art and Architecture)

The Persian kings exploited their huge empire in two main ways. They taxed the subject peoples with regular payments of tribute and they utilised their manpower in military expeditions to conquer new territories or to suppress revolts in those they already ruled. In several satrapies

lower-ranking Persians and Medians were granted small estates which provided them with modest revenues. In return they were expected to maintain themselves as cavalrymen, or charioteers, or to provide infantry soldiers for the king's armies. In years when such services were not demanded the estates were subject to taxes in silver or in kind, much like the rest of the land in the satrapy.

Surviving records show that the Persian Empire evolved a complex bureaucracy to administer the satrapies and dispose of their revenues according to the king's instructions. Members of the royal court and many other persons of importance were granted food and provisions from the royal storehouses. A system of roads linked together the major centres like Sardis, Ekbatana, Babylon, Susa and Persepolis. These roads were primarily for the use of soldiers and royal couriers,

This relief sculpture is from the royal palace at Persepolis, built in the late sixth and fifth centuries. It probably shows the two main builders of the palace, King Dareios I and his son and heir Xerxes. They have very long beards and wear square crowns. The flower-like objects carried by the king and his heir are probably bronze or golden lotus-blossom tokens. These would be handed out to members of the court as marks of favour at festivals. (Ancient Art and Architecture)

who were provided with way-stations, but the roads also facilitated the movement of trade and tribute across the empire. By the reign of Dareios, the Persian Empire was the largest the ancient world had ever seen. It stretched from the Balkans to the river Indus and its resources of wealth and manpower made the Great King the most powerful ruler in the ancient world.

The principal soldiers in all Persian armies were usually infantrymen who were Persians by birth and who carried large

shields, often made of leather and osier. They fought with a variety of weapons including long spears, axes, swords, and bows and arrows. Their armour was minimal, consisting at most of a padded cuirass of linen and perhaps a helmet, although most images show them wearing caps or hoods. The Persians were organised

A golden coin of the fifth century, known as a Daric, showing the king carrying a spear and a bow. This type of coin was introduced by King Dareios in the late sixth century. Coins were used throughout the ancient world to pay mercenaries. In the fifth and fourth centuries Persian gold played an increasingly important role in the political struggles of the Greeks, as the Persian kings used their enormous wealth to finance the wars of one Greek state against another. (Ancient Art and Architecture)

in regiments of 1,000 which could be grouped together in divisions of 10,000. The most important of these divisions was that of the 'Immortals', so called because casualties were always replaced to maintain the full complement of 10,000. The Immortals contained an élite regiment known as the King's Spearcarriers. This regiment was made up entirely of members of the Persian aristocracy. The conquest of Lydia in 547 demonstrated to Kyros the Great the need for a reliable corps of Persian cavalry, so he distributed conquered lands among the Persian nobles so that they could raise horses and fight as cavalry. The Persian kings also used Medes as cavalry and from the reign of Dareios onwards they recruited mercenary infantrymen and cavalrymen from the Saka tribes of central Asia. For major campaigns they levied troops from the subject peoples of the empire, gathering men from as far afield as Egypt and India, but the most reliable soldiers were always the Persians and the mercenaries from Iran and central Asia.

A gold bowl from Ekbatana. It is inscribed around the outside with the name of King Xerxes in three languages, Old High Persian, Akkadian and Elamite. Each of these is written in a cuneiform script, the style of writing developed in Mesopotamia in the fourth millennium. Akkadian was the language of the Babylonian kings. (Ancient Art and Architecture)

The rise of Sparta

The Greeks who confronted the might of the Persian Empire in the fifth century were mostly organised in small city-states. These communities varied in size, but they usually consisted of an urban centre, containing the major shrines and public buildings, surrounded by a rural territory, which was farmed by the male citizens, their families and slaves. The historical origins of these city-states are obscured by the layers of myths and legends with which later generations embellished the stories of their ancestors.

The Spartans were descended from a group of Greek-speaking tribes who had settled in a region called Lakonia, in the south-eastern Peloponnese, towards the end of the 11th century. About a hundred years later five villages in the broad plain of the river Eurotas amalgamated to form a single city, called Sparta. As part of the compromise involved in this arrangement it was decided that the new state would be ruled jointly by two royal families, the Agiadai and the Euryphontiai, each of which provided a king for the Spartans. These kings were advised by a council of elders, called the *gerousia*, whose membership was later restricted to 28.

The new city gradually exerted its influence over some of the surrounding communities and brought them under its control. Some were reduced to the status of slaves, but others retained a degree of autonomy. Their inhabitants were not fully integrated with the Spartans in social and political terms, but they fought alongside them in further campaigns of expansion and annexation. Their inhabitants became known as the *perioikoi*, meaning 'those who dwell around'. Towards the end of the eighth century the Spartans and their allies managed to defeat the inhabitants of Messenia, a wide, fertile region in the south-western Peloponnese, separated from the plain of Lakonia by the high ridges of Mount Taygetos. The Messenians proved to be difficult to dominate, however, and in the middle of the seventh century they rebelled against the Spartans and engaged them in a long, hard war. This war eventually ended in total victory for the Spartans, who took possession of Messenia and forced the inhabitants to become slaves. The former lands of the Messenians were divided into estates of roughly equal size and allocated to individual Spartan citizens, who did not live on the estates themselves but received up to half of their agricultural output as a form of rent. The Messenians themselves became known, like the Spartans' Lakonian slaves, as 'helots'.

Possession of the human and agricultural resources of Lakonia and Messenia enabled the Spartans to organise their community in a unique manner. The helots provided a servile workforce who furnished them with food and basic necessities, while the *perioikoi* engaged in manufacturing crafts and trading with the world outside Lakonia. This division of labour allowed the Spartan citizens to form an élite social and political group, called the Equals (*homoioi*). They were still ruled by their two kings, who acted as military commanders when the Spartans went to war. The Equals met in an assembly to vote upon major issues, such as whether or not to go to war, or make alliances with other states, but on a day-to-day basis their community came to be governed by five elected officials called 'ephors'. By the end of the sixth century the ephors had achieved a considerable degree of authority, even over the kings. The Equals devoted themselves to military training and gradually evolved into the most effective army in the Greek world. They perfected the art of hoplite warfare, fighting on foot in close formations using a large, round shield and a long thrusting spear. The Spartans became renowned for their courage and discipline and, because of this, they began to intervene in the political affairs of neighbouring city-states, usually at the invitation of one or other faction within that state. (See 'Portrait of a soldier' for a description of the Spartan educational and social system.)

During the seventh and sixth centuries many of the Greek city-states experienced

A bronze figurine of a Spartan hoplite, made in Lakonia in the sixth century. Items like this were frequently dedicated to the gods in temples across Greece, but hoplite figures are one of the commonest forms of dedication from Lakonia. This one has the typical pointed beard and long hair of a Spartan citizen. (Ancient Art and Architecture)

periods of social and political instability. The hereditary aristocracies who ruled them came under increasing pressure to share power and resources, above all agricultural land, which was the main source of wealth. For a while this pressure was eased by encouraging people to migrate overseas, particularly to Sicily, southern Italy and the northern Aegean, where many prosperous Greek communities had been established in the eighth and seventh centuries. Eventually the demands for political and social reform produced violent conflicts and in many city-states charismatic individuals emerged as leaders of the discontented elements. They overthrew the ruling groups and set themselves up as sole rulers. The Greeks used *tyrannos*, a word of Near-Eastern origin, to describe such men. It is usually translated as 'tyrant' in modern histories of ancient Greece, but it did not necessarily carry the overtones of oppressive or unpopular rule that the modern use of the term 'tyranny' implies. During the sixth century the Spartans overthrew many of these tyrannies, including those at Corinth, Sikyon, Naxos and Athens. They also attempted to overthrow Polykrates, the tyrant of Samos.

Athens before the Persian Wars

Athens was one of the largest of the Greek city-states. The city of Athens itself was the religious and political centre of an extensive territory comprising all the peninsula of Attika. Tradition held that the region had been unified under the kingship of the mythical hero Theseus, but by the middle of the seventh century the Athenians were governed by nine annually appointed officials, called 'archons', who were chosen from the males of a small group of

Tyrtaios describes the ideal Spartan hoplite

In the middle of the seventh century, when Spartans were struggling to overcome the rebellious Messenians, the Spartan poet Tyrtaios composed songs to exhort his fellow citizens to fight well. In the following extract (lines 21–38 of fragment 11) he gives a vivid, contemporary description of Greek hoplite warfare, which relied on the bravery and determination of infantrymen armed with a large shield and spear.

Let each man stand firm with his feet set apart, facing up to the enemy and biting his lip, covering his thighs and shins, his chest and shoulders with the wide expanse of his shield.
Let him shake his spear bravely with his right hand, his helmet's crest nodding fiercely above his head.
Let him learn his warfare in the heat of battle and not stand back to shield himself from missiles, but let him move in close, using his spear, or sword, to strike his enemy down.
Place feet against the enemy's feet, press shield against shield, nod helmet against helmet, so that the crests are entangled, and then fight your man standing chest to chest, your long spear or your sword in your hand.
And you, the light-armed men, hiding behind the shields, launch your sling-stones and javelins at them, giving good support to the heavy infantry.

In later years these poems became compulsory listening for Spartan armies. Tyrtaios also provided some additional encouragement for the lightly armed troops, who were normally recruited from helots or the *perioikoi*. See 'Portrait of a soldier' for more extracts from the poems of Tyrtaios.

aristocratic families. Many of the ordinary people of Attika resented the aristocrats' monopoly on power and their discontent encouraged an Athenian aristocrat called Kylon to attempt to set himself up as tyrant in 632. Kylon had been the victor in a chariot race at the Olympic Games, which implies that he was very wealthy, and he was married to the daughter of Theagenes, the tyrant of Megara. With Theagenes' help Kylon gathered a small band of followers and seized the Acropolis of Athens. His coup failed to attract wide support among the Athenians, many of whom joined in besieging Kylon and his men. Although Kylon and some of his immediate family escaped, the rest were forced to surrender and were subsequently killed. The causes of discontent remained, however, including aristocratic control of land, high rents and excessive use of debt-bondage, as well as the exclusion of many of the wealthier citizens from participation in government.

In 594 an aristocrat called Solon was chosen to revise the social and political structures of Athens. He reduced the problems of debt-bondage and opened up the archonship to wealthy non-aristocrats. He also established a people's council of 400 to widen participation in government. His reforms did not go far enough for many of the Athenians and they continued to quarrel over the right to govern the Athenian state. In 546, after two earlier failures, an aristocrat called Peisistratos, who had won great popularity as a military leader against the neighbouring state of Megara, set himself up as tyrant. He managed to remain in power until his death in 528, mainly by ensuring that the archons for each year were dominated by his supporters. His eldest son, Hippias, tried to continue the dynasty, but after his younger brother Hipparchos was murdered in 514 his rule became oppressive and unpopular. A leading aristocratic family, the Alkmaionidai, who had been closely involved in the defeat of Kylon's attempt at tyranny, bribed the Delphic oracle to persuade the Spartans to intervene. In 510 the Spartan king, Kleomenes, led an army

into Attika and deposed Hippias, who sought refuge with the Persian king, Dareios.

When he intervened in Athens, Kleomenes was following an established Spartan policy of deposing tyrants in other Greek states so that they could revert to the control of their aristocratic families and become allies of the Spartans. In the case of Athens, however, further quarrels among the leading families resulted in the creation of a different form of government. In 508/07 Kleisthenes of the Alkmaionidai was losing out in a power struggle with a rival aristocrat called Isagoras, but he attracted widespread support by promising radical reforms of the political system in Athens. In response Isagoras invited Kleomenes to lead a Spartan army into Attika and force Kleisthenes and his supporters into exile. The mass of Athenian citizens preferred the promised reforms to a continuation of aristocratic strife, so they eventually forced Kleomenes and his men to withdraw, taking Isagoras with them.

Kleisthenes was able to return to Athens and implement his programme of reform. He introduced a new organisational structure for the Athenians based on 140 local communities called 'demes'. All men over the age of 18 were registered as citizens through their deme and the demes were grouped into 10 newly created tribes, replacing the previous four tribes, which had been localised kinship units, dominated by certain aristocratic families. The demes offered an effective structure for local government. The tribes provided a mechanism for all citizens to become actively involved in running the state through a new council of 500 citizens who were appointed by selecting 50 men from each tribe by lot. This council discussed proposals for new laws and policies, but each proposal had to be put to a vote in the assembly before it could be implemented. All male citizens were entitled to attend this assembly and vote on the measures put before it, a principle of political equality, *isonomia*. One man from each tribe was elected to serve on a board of generals, who were both political and military leaders. To

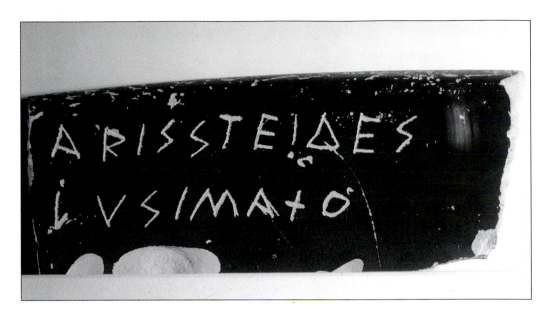

prevent more internal political conflicts of the kind that had led to his reforms, Kleisthenes also instituted a procedure for the citizen assembly to have the opportunity to vote once a year to banish a leading political figure for a period of 10 years. The voting was done by inscribing the name of the person on a piece of broken pottery, the Greek word for which was *ostrakon*; hence the process was known as ostracism.

Their new-found political unity and military strength encouraged the Athenians to assert themselves against other Greek states. They defeated their northern neighbours, the Boiotians, and took some territory from the city of Chalkis on the island of Euboia. They also began a long war against the island of Aigina for domination of the Saronic Gulf, but they lacked a large navy with which to challenge the Aiginetans at sea. Attika was a prosperous region with a growing population and some of the more adventurous aristocrats led expeditions to the Hellespont and other parts of the Aegean, where new settlements had been established during the rule of Peisistratos and his son. Some of these groups returned to Athens in the early fifth century as the region came under Persian influence during the reign of King Dareios.

This *ostrakon*, or potsherd, is inscribed with the name of Aristeides, the son of Lysimachos. The Athenians could vote once a year to exile a politician for 10 years by inscribing his name in this way. Aristeides was 'ostracised' in the late 480s, but returned to assist in the defeat of Xerxes in 480/79. A famously honest man, it is said that during the voting he was asked by an illiterate citizen who did not recognise him to write the name 'Aristeides' on an *ostrakon*, which he did, asking why the man wanted to exile him. 'I'm tired of hearing him being called Aristeides "the Just"', was the man's reply. (Ancient Art and Architecture)

Dareios sends an expedition to Greece

In 491 King Dareios of Persia sent envoys to the leading states of mainland Greece demanding that they submit to his rule by offering him symbolic gifts of earth and water. Many of them conceded to this demand, including the large island state of Aigina, but among those states that refused to acknowledge his authority were Athens and Sparta. In Athens the king's envoys were executed by being thrown into a pit normally used for the punishment of criminals. The Athenians may have been partly motivated by their own ongoing conflict with Aigina, their main maritime rival in the Saronic Gulf. It is possible that they had also learned of Dareios' intention to re-establish Hippias the son of Peisistratos as tyrant of Athens.

Dareios assembled an army in Kilikia and ordered his maritime subjects, including the Ionian Greeks, to prepare a fleet of warships and horse transports. This involved supplying tens of thousands of oarsmen to row the ships and providing some soldiers for the expedition, but the bulk of his army probably came from the Iranian heartlands of the Persian Empire. The figures given by the ancient sources for the size of the army, which range from 90,000 to 600,000 men, are clearly exaggerated, but it may have comprised around 25,000 soldiers, including 1,000 cavalry, and a fleet of up to 600 ships. The commanders of the expedition were Datis, a Median aristocrat who had been involved in the Persian counter-offensive against the Ionians in 494, and Artaphernes, son of the satrap of Lydia and the king's nephew.

The aim of this expedition was not the complete conquest of mainland Greece, for which a far larger force would be needed, but rather the establishment of a bridgehead on the eastern coast of Greece, preferably at Athens. Once this base was secured larger forces could be amassed for a full-scale invasion. The first target for the expedition was the island of Naxos, whose people wisely decided not to attempt to resist the Persians this time, but fled into the mountains, abandoning their city and temples to the enemy. Other islands in the Cyclades also made their submission and some contributed ships to the fleet of the Great King. The inhabitants of Euboia put up determined resistance, forcing the Persians to besiege the cities of Karystos and Eretria. The latter had contributed five ships to the ill-fated Ionian raid on Sardis in 498 and appealed to Athens for help. The Athenians had recently confiscated some land from another Euboian city, Chalkis, and settled 4,000 of their own citizens there. These men were instructed to march to Eretria and help defend the city, but on their arrival they discovered that the Eretrians were divided on the wisdom of continuing to oppose the Persians. So the settlers crossed over to Athens and avoided being caught in Eretria when Datis and Artaphernes arrived with their fleet and army, having persuaded the Karystians to surrender after only a few days. The Persians laid siege to Eretria and pressed their attack vigorously, with severe casualties on both sides. On the seventh day of the siege the pro-Persian faction in Eretria opened the gates. The inhabitants were made to pay for their earlier assistance in the Ionian Revolt; their city and temple were burned down and most of them were enslaved.

Having successfully achieved its initial objectives the expedition set sail for the coast of Attika. Given the casualties they had suffered while subduing Euboia and the need to leave strong detachments behind with Artaphernes to maintain control of the island, it is likely that the force which Datis led to Attika numbered less than

20,000 men. Datis' mission was to effect a
landing in Attika, capture the city of Athens
and restore the deposed tyrant Hippias to
power. Hippias, who accompanied the
Persians as a guide, adviser and potential
puppet ruler of Athens, advised Datis to take
the fleet across the narrow Euboian Strait
and land the army at the Bay of Marathon,
on the eastern coast of Attika. It was the
nearest suitable landing site to Eretria and
could provide ample water and pasturage.
The plain at Marathon was broad enough for
the deployment of the whole Persian army,

An Athenian red-figure painted jar of the mid-fifth
century. This unfortunate Persian soldier has used up all
his arrows, as the empty quiver on his belt shows. His
bow is now useless, although he hangs onto it in the
hope that he may recover some arrows. His only other
weapon is a curved sword, but it is insufficient against the
large shield and long spear of the Spartan hoplite
attacking him. (Ancient Art and Architecture)

including the cavalry, against any defending
forces. Hippias may also have expected to
receive a friendly welcome from the people
of eastern Attika, who had been strong
supporters of his father's tyranny.

The battle of Marathon

The Athenian generals decided to confront the Persians as soon they landed, rather than allow them to march on their city and then face a siege, as the Eretrians had done. They too may have been wary of the possibility of some of the citizens preferring to side with the invaders and the exiled tyrant Hippias, if they were allowed to establish themselves on Athenian territory. The Athenians assembled an army of about 9,000, mainly hoplite soldiers. They were joined by a further 600 or so men from the smaller city of Plataia, which lay north west of Attika and had been an ally of Athens for some 30 years. On hearing that the Persians had landed at Marathon they marched across the central plain of Attika and up the east coast to Marathon.

The Athenians and their Plataian allies took up a position on high ground, near to the road leading south from Marathon to Athens and awaited the Persians' next move. Herodotus says that there were protracted discussions among the Athenian commanders as to whether they should attack, but this may reflect embellishments made to the story of the battle in later years. It is more likely that the Greeks waited for the enemy to make a move. The Athenians and Plataians were heavily outnumbered and their generals will have been reluctant to move from their strong defensive position into the open plain of Marathon. To do so would have left them vulnerable to cavalry attacks and the possibility of being outmanoeuvred by the larger Persian force. It is also possible that the Athenians were waiting for the arrival of reinforcements from Sparta. Before they left Athens to march to Marathon the Athenians had sent their best runner, Philippides, to the Spartans with a request for aid. He covered the distance of approximately 140 miles in less than two days. The Spartans agreed to send a small army to help the Athenians, but their departure was delayed because they were in the middle of a major religious festival and had to wait until the full moon

signalled its completion. When they did set out, six days later, they marched with such great speed to Marathon that they arrived just three days later. Nevertheless, they were too late to participate in the battle, which had been fought on the previous day.

Herodotus' account describes a lengthy disagreement among the 10 Athenian generals, with half of them arguing that the size of the Persian force made it advisable to wait until they advanced, while the other half insisted that it was imperative to attack at once. According to Herodotus the impasse created by this equal division of opinions was broken by the intervention of Kallimachos, who held the office of *polemarchon*. In earlier times this official had been the commander of Athens' army, but under the new democratic constitution the army was commanded by a board of 10 elected generals, one from each of the 10 tribes. Kallimachos' position was more an honorary one, but he accompanied the army when it was engaged in fighting within the borders of Attika and he was entitled to a vote on major decisions. Herodotus says that one of the generals, Miltiades, persuaded Kallimachos to vote in favour of an attack by saying that further delay would mean victory for the Persians and slavery for the Athenians.

Herodotus also has Miltiades refer to the likelihood that continued inaction would breed dissension and fear among the Athenians, 'so that they will go over to the Medes'. This seems to be an indication that the decision to attack was taken in order to prevent treachery or defections. The presence among the Persians of Hippias, the former tyrant of Athens, provided one good reason to suspect that some of his supporters might choose to swap sides and

Persian infantrymen of the army division known as the Immortals. They wear long robes embroidered with regimental badges and are armed with a spear and a bow. This glazed brick relief of c.520 is from the palace of King Dareios at Susa, the original capital of the Median Empire. Dareios held his royal court there until his new palace in Persepolis became available. (Ancient Art and Architecture)

persuade others to follow them. The recent example of the betrayal of Eretria to the Persians was another. The longer the Athenians and Plataians were required to stand their ground and contemplate the strength of the enemy army, the easier it would be for them to believe that they could not defeat it and would be better off submitting to the rule of the Great King. It may also be that the Persian commander Datis had decided to wait for a sign that the enemy's resolve was weakening.

This tense stand-off lasted several days, during which no negotiations took place, nor was there even any skirmishing between the two sides. Eventually, the Athenian generals made the decision to attack the Persians. Several explanations have been offered for this bold decision. One possibility is that the Persians themselves formed up for battle and began to advance towards the Athenian position, with the intention of drawing them out onto the plain for a decisive battle. Certainly, if they wanted to march on Athens itself, the Persians had to remove the army, which was blocking the routes to the south and west. An alternative to this idea is the suggestion, made by a Byzantine scholar writing many centuries later, that the Athenians were informed by the Ionian Greeks among the enemy that parts of the Persian army, especially the cavalry, had begun to embark on their ships for a voyage around southern Attika to attack the city from the sea. Either way it seems probable that the Athenian advance was prompted by a change in the disposition of the Persian troops.

The Greeks attacked early in the day, perhaps while the Persian commanders were still getting their forces into position. Because the Persian army was spread out along a very wide front, the Athenians and their Plataian allies feared that they might be outflanked, so they extended the length of their own front, thinning out the ranks of their hoplites in the centre, but retaining a strong force on each wing. Datis positioned his best troops, a mixture of Persians and

TOP RIGHT The Persians landed on the beach in front of the marsh and made their camp to the north of the Kynosoura promontary. The Athenians and Plataians stationed themselves on high ground to the south, near the road to Athens. When Datis moved the Persians towards them and took up battle positions, the Greeks came down onto the plain and attacked. The Persians pushed back the centre of the Greek line, but their own wings were defeated and fled back towards their camp.

BOTTOM RIGHT Realising that their flanks were exposed, the Persian centre retreated, under attack on both sides from the victorious Greek wings. Most of the Persians forces reached the ships and escaped after fierce fighting at the ships, but many were hemmed in between the marsh and the beach and were killed.

Sakai, mercenaries from the regions north-east of Iran. His army included a large number of archers and slingers, as well as men equipped with javelins, whose function was to bombard the enemy from a distance with missiles before the other troops engaged them with spears, swords and axes.

As they faced each other on the plain the two armies were about a mile apart and the Greeks had to march across the open plain in order to engage the Persians. They completed most of this advance at a walking pace, but they ran the last 200 metres or so in order to reach the enemy before their own ranks were too heavily reduced by the arrows, javelins and slingstones. This decision to charge took the Persians by surprise. They seem to have underestimated their opponents' determination, which is not entirely surprising, given that they had recently overcome the Euboians and had been allowed to camp unchallenged on Athenian territory for several days. Nevertheless, they made ready to receive the charge, sending several volleys of missiles into the Greek ranks, with the aim of slowing or even halting the charge and then driving them back.

The Greeks closed the distance between the two armies as quickly as they could and they clashed across a broad front. In the centre, where the best Persian troops were concentrated, they pushed the Athenians back, pursuing them towards their original

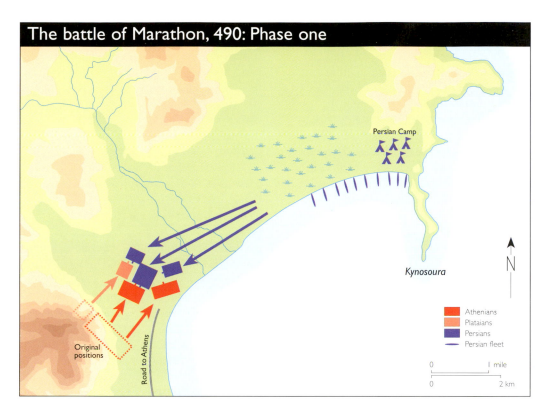

The battle of Marathon, 490: Phase one

Persian Camp

Kynosoura

N

Original positions

Road to Athens

■ Athenians
■ Plataians
■ Persians
— Persian fleet

0   1 mile
0   2 km

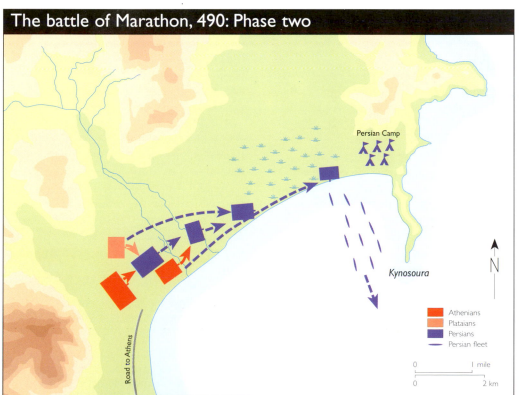

The battle of Marathon, 490: Phase two

Persian Camp

Kynosoura

N

Road to Athens

■ Athenians
■ Plataians
■ Persians
— Persian fleet

0   1 mile
0   2 km

camp. On the wings, however, the Athenians and the Plataians, who were concentrated on the left wing, succeeded in driving the Persian forces back and disrupting the cohesion and discipline of Datis' army. Under the pressure of the Greek onslaught the two wings of the Persians broke and fled back to their own camp. Realising that their flanks were now exposed and in danger of being surrounded by the victorious elements of the Greek army and attacked at the rear, the Persians and Sakai retreated as well. The Athenian and Plataian commanders gathered their forces together and fell upon them as they made their way back to their camp. There was not a complete rout, thanks to the discipline and experience of the Persian officers, who organised a rearguard and managed to embark many of their men onto the ships which were moored in shallow water just beyond the camp. Their casualties were high, however, with 6,400 men killed, many of them cut down as they crowded together, trapped between the sea, the pursuing Greeks and a marshy area to the north of the Persian camp. The Athenians lost only 192 men, including the *polemarchon* Kallimachos; Plataian casualties were also light.

Some modern scholars have been puzzled by the apparent lack of participation in the battle by the Persian cavalry. Herodotus does not mention them at all in his narrative of the action, which is the main reason why the Byzantine phrase about the cavalry embarking on the ships is taken seriously. The Persian cavalry was made up of a variety of ethnic units, including native Persians and subjects from other parts of the empire. Their main weapons were swords and spears, but they also used bows and arrows and javelins for hit-and-run attacks. It may well be that those Athenians who had survived the raid on Sardis and the subsequent retreat to Ephesos in 498 had exaggerated the threat posed by such cavalrymen. When pursuing heavy infantry, light cavalry would certainly have a major advantage, but in a battle fought at close quarters, over a relatively small area, the infantry would

have been far less vulnerable. If, as was their normal practice, the Persian commanders stationed their cavalry on the flanks of the main infantry formation, then they will have been driven back by the determined charge of the Greek hoplites and, with the extra speed and mobility that their horses provided, they may have been among the first to flee back to the ships.

Despite his defeat on the plain of Marathon, Datis, probably on the advice of Hippias, still felt that there was a chance to reach Athens by sea and capture it before the Athenian army could return. Accordingly he took his remaining men by sea around Cape Sounion and up to the Bay of Phaleron. Realising that the Persians were sailing south and heading for the city, the Athenians marched back as fast as they could and arrived in time to dissuade them from launching an assault. Herodotus reports the story that the Persians set off for Athens because they had received a signal, a polished shield flashing in the sun, which some Athenians claimed was given by members of the Alkmaionid family, but Herodotus himself does not believe this story and modern scholars have been inclined to agree with him. Unable to make any further progress against the Athenians, Datis sailed back to Asia Minor to report the failure of the expedition to the king.

The Athenians who died at Marathon were cremated and their ashes were buried in a funeral mound on the site of the battle. This mound, known as the Soros, still stands and is the approximate location of the main clash between the two armies. A force of 2,000 Spartans arrived on the battlefield the day after the battle. They inspected the Persian dead and praised the Athenians for

This bronze helmet is inscribed along the rim with the words: 'The Athenians, to Zeus, having taken this from the Medes.' It was captured as part of the booty, perhaps at the battle of Marathon in 490, and dedicated in the sanctuary of the god Zeus at Olympia. Dedications of captured arms and armour were an essential part of warfare for the Greeks, for whom they symbolised that victory had been won with the support and approval of the gods. (Ancient Art and Architecture)

The exterior of a red-figure painted wine cup, produced in Athens around 480. It features a Greek hoplite fighting at close quarters with a Persian infantryman. Both carry spears and shields, but the shields are of very different types. The round, concave Greek shield is made of wood covered with bronze and held by a hand-grip on the rim and an arm-grip in the centre. The rectangular, flat Persian shield is made of wicker and osiers and held by a single hand-grip in the centre. The hoplite also wears bronze armour, whereas his opponent is dressed in cloth and leather. (Ashmolean)

their victory before returning to Sparta. Once they were sure that the Persian forces were no longer a threat the Athenians celebrated their unexpected victory. It was the first time a Greek army had successfully overcome a Persian one. For the Athenians in particular it also represented a considerable triumph for their democratic citizen body. The ordinary Athenian (and Plataian) hoplites had defeated a larger, more

experienced and probably better disciplined
army in a magnificent display of solidarity,
bravery and sheer determination to defend
their homeland. From the Persian kings'
point of view the defeat at Marathon was a
serious setback for his campaign to punish
the Athenians and to conquer the Greek
states, but Marathon was far from the end
of the matter as far as the Persians were
concerned.

Xerxes' invasion of Greece

According to Herodotus, Dareios vowed to get revenge for the defeat of his army by the Athenians. Shortly after the news of Marathon reached him he ordered the best and bravest men in Asia to be levied for another campaign. That this levy was conducted for the sole purpose of subduing the Greeks is, however, unlikely, as there were many parts of the Persian Empire that also needed to be kept in line by strong military action. In 486 Dareios was called upon to deal with a revolt in one of the most troublesome provinces of the Persian Empire, Egypt. This satrapy had been conquered by his predecessor Kambyses in 525/24 and had remained under Persian control thereafter, even during the revolts and civil wars that characterised the first few years of Dareios' reign. Eventually the burden of tribute imposed by the Great King became too much for the Egyptians to bear and they attempted to drive the Persians out. Egypt was one of the wealthiest and strategically most important satrapies, so its revolt constituted a far greater threat to Dareios' power than the stubborn resistance of a few Greek cities. While Dareios was in Persia preparing for an expedition to bring the Egyptians back into line, he died of natural causes and was succeeded by his eldest son, Xerxes. The new king lost no time in crushing the Egyptian rebellion and asserting his authority as the 'king of all lands' and the favoured one of Ahuramazda. By 484 the whole of Egypt was once more under Persian control. Xerxes left his brother Achaimenes in charge as satrap of Egypt and returned to Persia.

Xerxes prepares to invade Greece

The Egyptian revolt was one of several problems that Xerxes inherited from his father. Babylonia, one of the central satrapies, also revolted in 481. Because of its position across the main communication routes between the eastern and western halves of the empire this satrapy was of even greater strategic importance than Egypt. Xerxes put down the revolt with considerable force and divided Babylonia into two smaller satrapies in an effort to make it easier to control. Another major concern for the son of Dareios was what to do about the Athenians and those other Greeks who had defied his father's demand to submit themselves to his authority. Although it is uncertain how much of Xerxes' military preparations in the first few years of his reign were directed towards the goal of defeating the Greeks, we can be sure that avenging the defeat at Marathon remained a high priority, and in 481 he was ready to move his armies westwards into Greece.

There are two facts that indicate the great importance that Xerxes attached to his invasion of Greece. Firstly, there is his decision to lead the expedition in person. By doing this he was following the precedents set by Kyros, Kambyses and Dareios, who all led major campaigns of imperial expansion to the west, against the Lydians, Egyptians and Ionians respectively. And as a new king he probably felt the need to show his nobles that he was a worthy successor to the renowned Dareios. Secondly, the sheer size and diversity of the forces that Xerxes assembled from all parts of his empire show that he intended this to be a great military triumph. It was, of course, meant to be primarily a Persian achievement, but one that was contributed to and witnessed by all the peoples who were subject to Persian rule.

Xerxes left Persia in the spring of 481 and headed for Sardis, the former capital of the kingdom of Lydia and the main administrative centre for Persian rule in western Anatolia. He assembled the bulk of his army there and then marched north-west to the Hellespont, which he crossed in early summer between Abydos and Sestos. From there he moved his army to Doriskos, which lay at the mouth of the river Hebros and was a suitable place to rest his forces. There was also a garrison fort there, originally established by his father Dareios in 512 when he was campaigning against the Skythians. Here at Doriskos, Herodotus says Xerxes held a review of his army and his fleet, which had been ordered to rendezvous with the army. Herodotus uses the occasion of this review to describe the different contingents of the Persian army and their sizes. As well as the usual core of Iranian infantry and cavalry, the Persians themselves, the Medes, and the Sakai, Herodotus says that the army comprised substantial contingents from other parts of Asia, including Baktrians, Babylonians and Kappadokians. Among the more exotic, and therefore questionable, groups that Herodotus says were present he lists a detachment of camel-riding troops from Arabia and some primitive infantry from the depths of Ethiopia. The king's Ionian Greek subjects were also required to furnish men for the army, in the shape of hoplites, but their main contribution, like that of the Egyptians, Kilikians and Phoenicians was to the navy. In general Xerxes seems to have taken a high proportion of archers and other missile troops, as well as a great deal of cavalry.

The size of Xerxes' army presents historians with an awkward problem. According to Herodotus the army consisted of 1,800,000 troops levied in Asia, plus a further 300,000 from the parts of Europe that the army marched through on its way to Greece, giving a grand total of 2,100,000. In addition he claims that there were over 2,600,000 servants, attendants and other camp-followers, giving a

combined force of over 4,700,000, without including the personnel of the fleet. The numbers that Herodotus gives are clearly an exaggeration, no doubt resulting from a contemporary historical tradition that magnified the success of the defence of Greece by multiplying the numbers of the enemy. The size of Xerxes' army is, therefore, very difficult to establish. Modern scholars disagree widely on how much to reduce the figure for the land army. Some put the number as low as 50,000, but a more generous estimate is 200,000. Possibly the true figure lies somewhere between these two, at around 100,000–150,000 fighting men, but a definitive answer to the question eludes us.

It is somewhat easier to believe the numbers offered by Herodotus for the size of the naval forces because ships were much easier to count than soldiers. Observers standing on a shoreline and watching a fleet sail past them would have a reasonable chance of accurately counting each individual vessel. Alternatively if, as some scholars maintain, Herodotus or his sources had access to official Persian records of the forces involved in the expedition, it is much more likely that the numbers for the various sections of the fleet were given precisely, whereas the contingents of the army may have been listed in general terms, rather than given as exact figures. Herodotus tells us that, at its greatest size, Xerxes' fleet numbered 1,207 trireme warships, and was accompanied by over 3,000 transport and supply ships. In spite of the comments made above, there are some difficulties posed by these numbers, which seem very large, even if they are assumed to represent the total capacity of the Persian navy. Herodotus claims there were over 250,000 oarsmen and sailors on these ships, but it may be that some of the vessels were manned by only skeleton crews, or even towed behind other ships to provide reserve vessels. Certainly it was a common procedure later in the fifth century for naval commanders to concentrate their manpower on their best and fastest warships prior to a battle.

The range and diversity of the peoples of the Persian Empire is indicated by this fifth-century black-figure painted vase from Athens. It shows two Negro soldiers with clubs and shields fighting a Greek hoplite. Ethiopian units were part of the army that Xerxes assembled for the invasion of Greece in 480. Many also fought on board the Egyptian ships of the Persian fleet. (Ancient Art and Architecture)

Whatever the numbers were, it is clear that Xerxes was anxious to ensure his expedition was successful, and he reasoned that mustering an overwhelming numerical superiority by land and sea was the best way to do it.

From Asia Minor to Greece

Xerxes ordered extensive preparations to be carried out along the route of the expedition, from western Asia Minor to northern Greece. In order for his army to cross the Hellespont from Asia into Europe two pontoon bridges were built. They spanned one of the narrowest sections of the straits, between the cities of Abydos and Sestos. To create each bridge several hundred warship hulls were anchored at right angles to the prevailing currents and linked together by six heavy cables. Between these cables planks of wood were laid to make a continuous platform, and then a causeway was constructed on top of the platform out of earth and brushwood. Finally a fence was built up on either side of the causeway, so that those animals crossing the bridges, horses, mules, oxen and camels, would not see the water and take fright. These bridges will have saved a great deal of time, for the process of embarking and disembarking such a huge army on transport ships would have taken many days, and unfavourable weather might have resulted in further loss of time. Even so the weather almost wrecked the whole scheme, as a storm blew up while the bridges were under construction and wrecked both of them. Xerxes' anger led him to execute the men supervising the work and, in what may seem to us a rather bizarre ritual, he had the waters

of the Hellespont symbolically whipped and branded, as though they were a recalcitrant slave.

From Doriskos, the army and navy progressed along the coast of Thrace towards Macedonia, meeting up at various pre-arranged points along the way. By co-ordinating the movements of the fleet and navy in this way Xerxes and his commanders sought to guard against the possibility of the Greeks making seaborne raids on his land forces and supply depots and also to ensure that safe havens were available for his fleet once it moved into hostile waters. Initially the paths of the fleet and army lay quite close together, but they separated near Akanthos in order to follow distinct routes. Xerxes was determined that his fleet would not fall victim to the dangerous north-Aegean storms that had wrecked the ships commanded by Mardonios in 492 as they attempted to sail round the headland of Mount Athos. He therefore ordered the cutting of a canal through the low-lying plain at the narrowest part of the peninsula, near the city of Akanthos. There are still some traces of this canal visible today.

The two elements were reunited at Therme, a small town at the head of the Thermaic Gulf. Xerxes then led the army southwards into northern Greece, passing through the lower reaches of the kingdom of Macedon and from there into the open plains of Thessaly. The Macedonians had enjoyed friendly relations with the Persians since the days of Dareios, whose campaigns against the Skythians had reduced the threat to Macedon from its northern neighbours. The Macedonian king, Alexander I, allowed Xerxes to prepare a supply depot on his territory and he contributed some infantry to the ever-growing ranks of the Persian army. The supply depot was part of a series of such bases established along the marching route through Thrace and Macedonia. One of the most impressive achievements of the whole march from Sardis to central Greece is that Xerxes' commanders managed to keep feeding and watering their men and animals. An army of over 100,000 men would have required many tons of food and water, as would their draught animals, horses and camels. It might be thought that the large Persian fleet was supposed to supply the army by carrying food and fodder from one staging point to the next, but the sheer size of the fleet would have made this an impractical idea. The 1,207 trireme warships alone would have carried at least 200,000 oarsmen and sailors, even if it is assumed that many of them were not fully crewed. The 3,000 or so other vessels that Herodotus says accompanied the warships would not have needed such large crews, and their purpose would have been to carry sufficient supplies to keep the fleet provisioned, but not the army.

Some food will have been transported with the army, using draught animals, including camels, as well as some human porters. Supplies of fresh water will have been collected and carried from one camp to the next, but only in small quantities. Ensuring a constant supply of water was always a very high priority for ancient armies. Herodotus claims that Xerxes' men and animals were so numerous they drank whole streams and rivers dry, but this is no doubt another picturesque exaggeration that we should not take too seriously. Nevertheless, finding and distributing adequate supplies of fresh water must have been one of the most difficult tasks faced by the men charged with keeping the army and navy going, especially in the latter stages of the campaign when they were passing through parts of northern and central Greece, where large rivers are rare and many

The 'Strangford Shield' is a Roman copy of the shield held by the statue of Athena that was housed in the Parthenon, the largest of the temples on the Athenian Acropolis. The statue was covered with ivory and gold that could be removed and used to pay wartime expenses. Although Athens was rich by the standards of the Greek states of the fifth century, her wealth was small in comparison with that of the Persian Empire. (Ancient Art and Architecture)

watercourses dry up naturally in the summer. In practice the details of the marching route will have been largely determined by the location of adequate sources of drinking water.

When it came to finding food a very heavy burden was laid upon the inhabitants of those territories through which the army and the fleet passed on their long journey. The Thracians and Macedonians in particular were expected to provide food for the army and to allow the animals to graze on their meadows. At each stage of the march the army camped around a huge tent erected for Xerxes and his closest followers, mainly Persian and Median nobles, who expected to be served from vessels of silver and gold. According to the accounts of the islanders of Thasos, whose possessions on the mainland obliged them to contribute, the combined cost of entertaining Xerxes and his court in the accustomed luxury as well as supplying the bread and meat needed for the soldiers and the grain for the animals for just one day came to the enormous sum of 400 talents of silver. Megakreon, one of the leading citizens of Abdera, is said to have remarked to his compatriots that they should be thankful Xerxes only took one main meal in the day, otherwise they would have been forced to abandon their city altogether rather than try to cater for his army twice in a day.

Even if their resources were not up to the task, these peoples will have had no alternative but to acknowledge their obligations to Xerxes as their overlord and supply as much as they could. Xerxes' forces were too large for the tribal and city leaders of the region to confront directly and the fact that he was clearly intent on passing

The inside of a red-figure painted wine cup, made in Athens around 480. The artist has portrayed a young man putting the finishing touches to a bronze helmet of the Corinthian type. The helmet was made from a single sheet of bronze, heated and beaten into the appropriate shape. Helmets of this type were commonly worn by Greek hoplites in the early fifth century, but they were gradually replaced by lighter helmets that allowed better vision and hearing.. (Ancient Art and Architecture)

through, rather than stopping to assert control over their territories will have encouraged them to do everything they could to speed the Persians on their way. The prospect of joining such a massive army of invasion for the sake of sharing in its plunder of the Greeks may also have contributed to the readiness with which the peoples of the northern coast of the Aegean submitted to the Great King. Xerxes made a point of gathering these additional forces under his command to emphasise that their homelands were part of his empire. Consequently there were no attempts to challenge the army or the fleet as they made their way towards Greece, although Herodotus does mention that some of the camels were attacked by lions as the army was passing through Macedonia.

The Greeks prepare to defend themselves

In Greece the reaction to the news that the Persian king was preparing a large invasion force was mixed. Many of the Greek city-states banded together into a league which modern historians have called the Hellenic League, because the ancient Greeks used the word *Hellenes* to describe themselves. One of the most significant aspects of the initial meeting of this league in 481 was that the member states agreed to end any conflicts with each other and swore an oath to be allies permanently. Hence Athens and Aigina, two of the members who had been at war with each other for over 20 years, now became firm allies in order to resist the Persians. The Spartans were appointed the commanders of the League forces, by both land and sea, in spite of a suggestion that the Athenians should head the naval contingents. Spies were sent to Asia Minor to find out more about Xerxes' preparations, and envoys were sent to some of the more powerful Greek states and confederations across the Mediterranean to ask for help.

It is clear that by no means all the major Greek city-states joined the League, but its precise membership is difficult to establish. Herodotus gives a list of those Greeks who 'medised', that is, they submitted to the Persian king and gave him symbolic presents of earth and water to acknowledge his authority over them, but he includes many states that were originally members of the Hellenic League, such as the Thessalians, the Thebans and the Phokians. These states only surrendered to Xerxes after his army overran their territory and they were abandoned by their allies, whereas Argos, a bitter enemy of Sparta simply refused to have anything to do with an alliance under Spartan leadership. Some of the other Greek states accused the Argives of already being committed to helping Xerxes. The Argives did not provide any actual assistance to the Persians, but it may be that they were awaiting the outcome of the conflict with the Hellenic League *before* committing themselves.

Another state that refused to help was Syracuse, whose ruler Gelon was leading a Sicilian confederation in a war to resist the increasing influence of the Carthaginians in Sicily. The association of Cretan cities also refused to send any assistance. The prosperous island state of Korkyra (modern Corfu) did dispatch a force of 60 ships in response to the Hellenic League's appeal, but they got no further than the southern coast of the Peloponnese and played no part in the actual fighting. It is possible that the Corcyreans, like the Argives, decided to play a waiting game and not get involved in the conflict until it was clear that one side was victorious.

In the early summer of 480, at about the time that Xerxes and his army were crossing the Hellespont, the principal ruling family of Thessaly, the Aleudai, were preparing to welcome him, having committed themselves to the Persians as early as 492. There were some dissident groups among the Thessalians who did not support this policy and they requested that the Hellenic League send a force to oppose the Persians at the border between Thessaly and Macedonia. An army of 10,000 League hoplites, under the command of Euainetos the Spartan, marched to the valley of the river Peneus at Tempe, the main pass into Thessaly from lower Macedonia. After only a few days they abandoned this position and left the Thessalians with no alternative but to submit to Xerxes. The League commander seems to have decided that there were too many alternative routes into Thessaly that Xerxes could use to outflank the pass at Tempe. It is noteworthy that the Hellenic League forces had been transported by sea as far as the Gulf of Pagasai, on the southern edge of Thessaly. The intention was probably to station their own fleet there against the possibility that the Persians might try to sail around and land forces at their rear.

Opinion in the Hellenic League was now divided between the Peloponnesian members, like Sparta and Corinth, who advocated retreating as far as the narrow Isthmus of Corinth, and the non-Peloponnesian states like Thebes and Athens, who argued that their territories should not be abandoned without a fight. It was decided to make a stand in central Greece at a very narrow passage of land between the mountains and the sea called Thermopylai, meaning 'hot gates', so called because of its hot sulphurous springs. It was virtually the only route from Thessaly into central Greece that could be used by Xerxes' huge army and it was chosen as the best defensive position available. A small army was sent to occupy the pass and a fleet was assembled to take up a position at Artemision on the northern end of the island of Euboia. The fleet would prevent the Persians from landing troops along the coastline at the rear of the Greek army at Thermopylai. The overall command of these forces was taken by Leonidas, one of the Spartan kings, and the naval contingent was placed under the direction of another Spartan called Eurybiades.

The army sent to Thermopylai was made up of about 8,000 hoplites, very few of whom were Spartans. The main Lakonian contingent of about 1,000 was probably drawn from the *perioikoi*. Leonidas was accompanied by a picked bodyguard of 300 Spartan citizens, chosen for their bravery and determination, and because they each had living sons whom they left behind in Sparta. As was usual they were accompanied by personal helot servants, who could also participate in the fighting as light-armed troops. There were 2,800 other Peloponnesians present, mainly from the cities of Arkadia, the region to the north of Lakonia, and the rest of the troops came from central Greece, principally the regions of Malis, Phokis, eastern Lokris and Boiotia. The reason Herodotus gives for the small number of Spartans is the same one that explained their delay in reaching Marathon ten years earlier. They were celebrating an important religious festival, the Karneia, and could not leave Sparta until it was finished. The limited number of other Peloponnesians is also accounted for by a religious commitment, although in their case it was the four-yearly Olympic festival which kept many of them away. Some scholars have suggested a less noble reason, however, which is that the Peloponnesian states were reluctant to commit their manpower to the defence of central Greece, preferring to keep their man strength closer to home.

Nevertheless, there were many other Greeks involved in the joint land and sea operation. Herodotus says that the Greek fleet at Artemision numbered 271 triremes. The principal naval resources of the Greeks were the trireme fleets of Athens, Corinth and Aigina. If, as in later years, each of these carried 170 oarsmen and 30 sailors and marines, there would have been around 54,000 men in the fleet, including at least 10 hoplites and four archers per ship, making a total of nearly 4,000 soldiers. The strong Athenian presence was the result of a very recent ship-building programme. In 488/87 the Athenians were

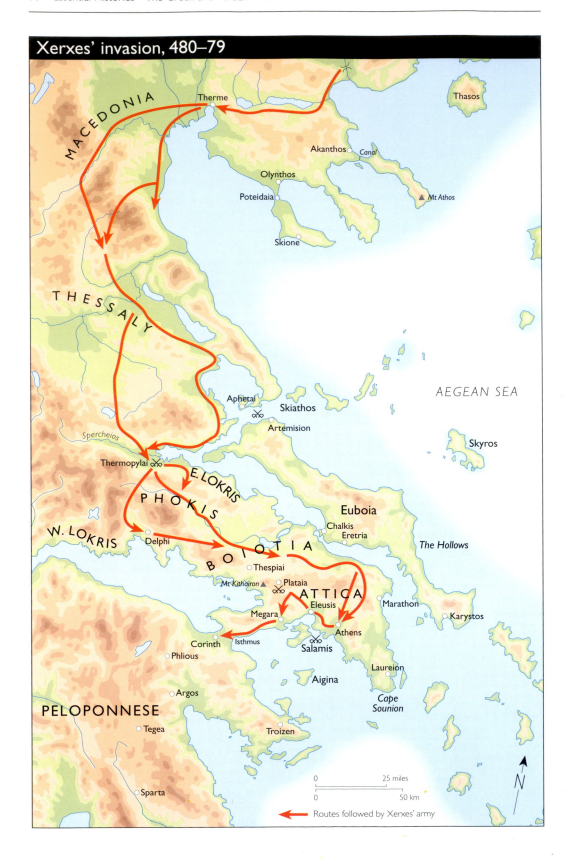

Xerxes' invasion, 480–79

Thasos

Therme

MACEDONIA

Akanthos · Canal

Olynthos

Poteidaia

▲ Mt Athos

Skione

THESSALY

Spercheios

AEGEAN SEA

Aphetai

Skiathos

Artemision

Skyros

Thermopylai

E. LOKRIS

PHOKIS

Euboia

W. LOKRIS

Delphi

Chalkis
Eretria

The Hollows

BOIOTIA

Thespiai

Mt Kithoiron ▲

Plataia

ATTICA

Megara

Eleusis

Marathon

Karystos

Corinth · Isthmus

Athens

Phlious

Salamis

Laureion

Aigina

Argos

Cape
Sounion

PELOPONNESE

Tegea

Troizen

Sparta

| 0 | | 25 miles |
| 0 | | 50 km |

⟶ Routes followed by Xerxes' army

N

so short of vessels for their war against the island of Aigina that they had to buy some old warships from Corinth. In 483 the Athenians received a financial windfall from the discovery of a very rich silver vein in the public mines at Laureion. An ambitious politician called Themistokles persuaded them not to distribute the profits among the citizens, but to invest them in a new fleet of triremes. By 480 they had 200 warships, making them the largest naval contributors to the Hellenic League. They were keen that one of their generals should be appointed to command the Greek fleet, but Sparta's numerous allies insisted on a Spartan commander.

The Persians approach Thermopylai and Artemision

The pass of Thermopylai was, in ancient times, a narrow strip of land where the main route between Thessaly and central Greece is bordered by high mountains on one side and the sea on the other. It was barely 15 metres across in its central section, known as the Middle Gate, where there had been an old defensive wall built by the Phokians. Leonidas ordered some of his men to rebuild this to add to the strength of the position. He chose this point to make his main stand because, although the pass was even narrower at its two ends (the East and West Gates), the mountain slopes were much gentler at those points and could be scaled by large bodies of men. On his arrival he was told by some of the local Malians that there was a route through the mountains to the south of Thermopylai which rejoined the main route at the East Gate. It was known as the Anopaia path. As this pathway also branched off southwards into the territory of Phokis he placed the Phokian hoplites midway along it, preventing the Persians from using it to outflank his position and attack his army from the rear.

Xerxes' army crossed the river Spercheios and camped near the town of Trachis, to the

west of Thermopylai, at the end of August 480. It took several days for the entire army to assemble and for the Persians to scout the enemy positions and report back to the king and his commanders. On seeing the enormous size of the Persian army now marshalled against him, Leonidas sent an urgent message to the states of the Hellenic League asking for reinforcements. Rumours of the huge forces being prepared by Xerxes for his invasion of Greece must have been circulating for some time before the Persians reached Greece. Herodotus says that three Greek spies were sent to Asia Minor to gather information. They observed the marshalling of Xerxes' forces at Sardis, but were captured and were about to be executed when Xerxes himself intervened and ordered them to be taken around the camp and shown all the contingents of infantry and cavalry, in order to impress upon them the overwhelming superiority of his army. Like so many of the anecdotes passed on by Herodotus this one is not easy to believe, but even if the Greek spies were given a guided tour of the army at Sardis, it is unlikely that these reports and rumours would have been given full credence by the Greek leaders until they could confirm them with their own eyes. Despite the daunting size of the Persian army Leonidas seems to have been fairly confident that his force of 8,000 men was adequate for the task of holding the pass temporarily, but he felt the need for further troops to shore up the defence over a longer period. It was later said that Xerxes, in an attempt to avoid a battle, offered Leonidas the chance to join his army and become his satrap of Greece, but Leonidas refused, saying that it was better to die for the freedom of the Greeks than to live and rule them.

As the Persian army reached Thermopylai, the fleet made its way from Therme to Aphetai on the southern tip of the peninsula of Magnesia, encountering three advance scout ships from the Greek fleet and capturing two of them. Severe

A bronze statuette of a warrior, dedicated in the sanctuary of Zeus at Olympia in the western Peloponnese in the sixth century. By the time of Xerxes' invasion, Olympia was one of the most important sanctuaries in the Greek world and the famous Olympic festival, held every four years, attracted thousands of celebrants from across the Mediterranean. The athletic competitions at the festival included a race for men wearing bronze helmets and carrying hoplite shields. (Ancient Art and Architecture)

losses were incurred by the Persians when they put into the shore on the eastern side of Magnesia en route. A storm blew up and wrecked nearly a third of the Persian ships. Eventually the survivors made it to Aphetai and prepared to engage the Greeks at sea.

The size of the Persian fleet that gradually assembled at Aphetai after the storm must also have come as something of a shock to the Greeks. Before it was hit by the storm the Persian fleet numbered 1,207 triremes and about 3,000 other vessels. It will have taken a long time, possibly several days, to settle into its new anchorage. At this point the Greeks debated abandoning their position at Artemision and heading south. Herodotus claims that it was only through bribery that the principal Greek commanders, the Athenian, Themistokles, the Spartan, Eurybiades, and the Corinthian, Adeimantos, were persuaded to remain and continue with the co-ordinated strategy of stopping the Persian advance by land and sea. The Greeks had 271 triremes and about 50 other ships. They were later joined by 53 Athenian triremes, which seem to have been part of the Athenians' reserve forces, held back to guard Attika, but they were apparently sent north, perhaps in response to a plea for reinforcements similar to that which Leonidas sent after seeing the size of Xerxes' army. The Persians' advantage in numbers was potentially overwhelming, a fact that would have been obvious to the Greeks while they observed or received reports on the build-up of Persian forces at Aphetai.

The Persians were well informed about the size of their opponents' naval forces,

mainly as a result of their early success in capturing two Greek triremes and their crews. According to Herodotus the Persians expected the smaller Greek force to sail away under the cover of night, so, after the king's fleet had assembled at Aphetai, they held off from attacking the Greeks until a squadron of 200 ships, which had been dispatched southwards to circumnavigate Euboia and prevent the Greeks from escaping, signalled that it was in position. Although the basic idea seems credible enough, there are some problems in accepting all of what Herodotus says about this stratagem. He suggests that the ships took a route beyond the island of Skiathos in order to avoid being observed as they journeyed round Euboia, but this seems unlikely to have worked, since there were Greek observers on Euboia who would surely have spotted the Persians as they started out and could even have monitored their progress at several points en route. It is more likely that they would have separated from the main fleet before they reached Aphetai, although even then they could not have expected to avoid detection throughout their voyage, which, at a distance of over 400 kilometres, would probably have taken several days to complete. The move was presumably part of a plan to trap the Greek ships between the two elements of the Persian fleet and capture or destroy them. A further question arises as a result of these considerations, namely, how could the Persians co-ordinate the two sections of their fleet? Herodotus clearly says that the main force at Aphetai was not supposed to engage the Greeks until it had seen the signal that announced the approach of the 200 ships sent round Euboia. The plan was probably to allow a certain amount of time, perhaps three or four days, for the 200 ships to complete their voyage, after which the main fleet could assume that they were in position and begin to drive the Greeks away from Artemision and into the trap. The initial reluctance of the Persians to attack the Greeks at Artemision, at least for two days, is thus explained by the need to give their flanking force time to get into position. Given what Herodotus says about their expectation that the Greeks would flee, they may even have expected to be informed of the 200 ships' successful circumnavigation of Euboia by the enemy's panicked withdrawal.

While the Persians were assembling their main force at Aphetai, the Greeks captured 15 ships that had got detached from the rest of the fleet and sailed into the Greek base at Artemision by mistake. It was probably from the commanders of these ships that the Greeks learnt of the Persian plan to send a squadron round Euboia, although Herodotus recounts the story of Skyllias of Skione, a Greek diver employed by the Persians, who supposedly swam across the straits from Aphetai to Artemision to warn the Greeks of the Persian plan. Some of the Greek captains were in favour of avoiding battle until nightfall and then heading back to meet these 200 ships well to the south. Eventually Eurybiades decided that his forces were strong enough to challenge the Persian fleet, which was still recovering from the earlier storm damage. The Greeks sailed out to attack while the Persian land forces were beginning to engage their compatriots holding the pass at Thermopylai. The Persian fleet comfortably outnumbered the Greeks, and its commanders responded to the challenge. The two fleets met in relatively open water and the Persians immediately began to encircle the Greeks, hoping to close in on them and use boarding tactics to capture their ships. They carried far more fighting men than the Greek ships, including detachments of Persian, Median or Sakai soldiers. The Greek ships stayed close together in a circular formation to avoid being set upon one by one and overwhelmed, but they gradually crowded in on each other so much that they had to risk a mass breakout through the enemy lines. After some brief ramming action, in which the Greeks excelled because their less heavily manned ships were lighter and faster, 30 Persian vessels

were captured. A ship from the Greek island of Lemnos also defected from the Persian side. Eurybiades withdrew for the night and sent a message to Leonidas saying that he would hold his position for another day.

Overnight the Persian detachment of 200 ships that was making its way round Euboia was caught in yet another bad storm at a place called 'the Hollows' and was completely destroyed. Not only did this cancel out any chance of trapping the Greeks between two sections of the fleet, it also reduced the overall numerical advantage that the Persians enjoyed. The 53 Athenian ships that arrived at this point also helped to redress the balance a little. When the Greeks learnt of their good fortune they went on the offensive again and launched a swift attack on the Persians, who were still waiting for a sign that their detachment had completed its journey. Several Kilikian ships were sunk and Eurybiades again told Leonidas that he was could hold out another day.

The battle of Thermopylai

The Greek defence of the pass of Thermopylai lasted three days. Initially the Persians seem to have thought that they could overwhelm the Greeks by sheer weight of numbers, but the extreme narrowness of the central section of the pass made it impossible for them to make effective use of their superior numbers. Xerxes himself was particularly contemptuous of the small Greek army. He is said by Herodotus to have sent two Median divisions (about 20,000 men) forward with orders to capture the Greeks and bring them to the king. When the Medes retreated after losing many men he ordered Hydarnes, commander of the élite Persian division known as the Immortals to take up the battle. But even his best soldiers could not overcome the determined resistance of the Greeks. It seems likely that Leonidas and his small Spartan force

The battle of Thermopylai, 480

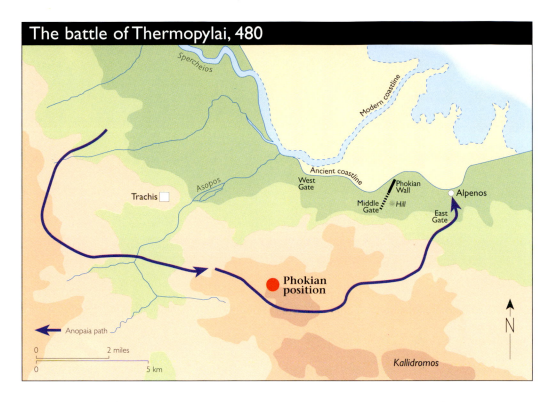

initially bore the brunt of the attack, but the Greeks rotated their forces so that they were able to rest many of their contingents and regularly deploy fresh men into the front line of the battle. The large, round shields and long thrusting spears of the Greek hoplites were very effective in this kind of close-quarter fighting and the Spartans had developed good tactics for drawing the enemy into the fight. They would feign a retreat and, as the enemy pressed forward, confident of victory, they would turn about and engage them face to face.

Towards the evening of the second day of fighting, Xerxes, impatient to remove the Greek forces and carry on into the heart of Greece, ordered Hydarnes to take the Immortals over the treacherous Anopaia path over the mountains and attack Leonidas and his men from the rear. The pathway through the mountains was a difficult one to traverse even in daytime, but at night there was increased danger. Fortunately for the Persians a local man from Trachis, Ephialtes, son of Eurydemos,

came forward in the hope of receiving a substantial reward from Xerxes. He offered to show them the path and guide them along it and back down to the eastern entrance of the pass. Hydarnes and his men set off at sundown and made their way along the mountain track towards the East Gate of the pass. As it was getting light the Persians encountered the 1,000 Phokians who had been positioned there to guard against just such a move. At first Hydarnes was afraid that they were more Spartans, but he was reassured by Ephialtes that they were not. The Phokians heard the Persians approaching but they had little time to prepare. Assuming that the Persians were intent on engaging them, as soon as the arrows started flying they retreated to a better defensive position on a nearby hilltop, ready to fight to the death. Hydarnes was too experienced a commander to let this opportunity slip by and he ordered his men to pay no further attention to the Phokians but to carry on towards the pass.

This dynamic bust of a Spartan warrior from the fifth century is thought by some to be a portrait of the heroic Spartan king, Leonidas, who died at the battle of Thermopylai. It certainly captures the sense of resolution that enabled Leonidas and his small force to continue to oppose the huge army of Xerxes after their position became hopeless. (Ancient Art and Architecture)

Leonidas had a few hours' warning of the approach of the Persians from some scouts who had been stationed with the Phokians to report any enemy movements. Leonidas now had to make a crucial decision whether to continue his defence of the pass, or to abandon it and retreat southwards. Some of Herodotus' informants claimed that many of the Greeks did not even wait for their commander to make up his mind, but fled as soon as they heard that the Persians were on their way. Herodotus is more inclined to believe that they were ordered to depart by Leonidas who realised that the Greek force was no longer capable of holding the pass now that the enemy could attack from two sides. In the event not all of the Greeks retreated because Leonidas and his 300 picked Spartans stayed behind, along with some of the Boiotians, namely 400 Thebans, whom some Greeks later claimed were kept there by Leonidas as hostages, and 700 hoplites from Thespiai.

Leonidas' decision to keep a small force in place is difficult to understand in strategic terms. The force was now too small to cause much delay to the progress of the Persians; though it might have been intended as a rearguard to cover the retreat of the rest of the Greeks. If so, it was a brave gesture to fight to the death against the invaders, belying the suggestion that the Spartans were not committed to the defence of the rest of the Greeks. Herodotus was told of an oracle given to the Spartans by the priestess of Apollo at Delphi at the start of the campaign, which said that the Spartans must lose either their city or their king to the Persians. Leonidas had become king rather unexpectedly, because he had two older brothers who both predeceased him. It may be that he felt he needed to do

something brave and honourable to justify his position as king, or it may be that there really had been a prophecy suggesting that the death of a king would save the city of Sparta, but we cannot hope to know his reasons. The decision of the Boiotians to remain behind and fight to the death with Leonidas and his men shows that the Spartans were not the only Greek hoplites who could be brave in the face of overwhelming odds.

While the rest of the Greeks retreated and a messenger was sent by ship to the fleet at Artemision to tell Eurybiades that the defence of the pass was over, Leonidas led the remaining hoplites forward to engage the enemy. Xerxes' main army was urged on by the officers, some of whom used whips to drive their more reluctant soldiers into battle. The result was a fierce and bloody combat in which many Persians fell, some trampled by their own comrades. The hoplites initially fought with their spears, but when these were broken they used their short swords. Among the casualties were two of Xerxes' half-brothers, presumably fighting in the front ranks of the Persians. Finally Leonidas himself fell and his body then became a prize fought over by the Spartans and the Persians. When Hydarnes and the Immortals emerged from the Anopaia pathway and approached the rear of the Greeks, the Spartans, their surviving helots and Thespiaians moved to a small hill behind the Phokian wall and made a last stand there, fighting with swords, bare hands and even teeth, until the Persians drew back and slew the last of them with arrows. Some of the Thebans managed to separate themselves and surrender, but the Persian king was ill-tempered in victory. He enslaved the Thebans and branded them with his royal symbol; their city had submitted to him, but they had joined his enemies. He also had the body of Leonidas impaled and decapitated, so enraged was he with the Spartan king's defiance. According to Herodotus, Leonidas and his army had cost Xerxes 20,000 men.

The Greeks later honoured Leonidas and his fallen comrades with a monument and several verse epitaphs, one of which was for Megistias, a seer and diviner from Akarnania in western Greece who accompanied Leonidas. He was said to have predicted that disaster was about to happen when he examined the sacrificial animal that was slaughtered in the early hours of the morning, as Hydarnes and the Immortals were making their way through the mountains. Leonidas offered him the chance to join the retreat, but he refused, sending his son away instead. The epitaph was composed by his friend, the poet Simonides:

In remembrance of the renowned Megistias,
slain by the Medes when they crossed the river
Spercheios; although the seer saw clearly his
impending fate, he did not choose to abandon
the Spartan leader.

Ephialtes, the local man who had guided the Persians through the mountains and behind the Greeks fled to Thessaly, fearing that the Spartans would take their revenge upon him. A price was put on his head and although he was eventually killed in a private quarrel by another man from Trachis, the Spartans nevertheless rewarded his killer.

The evacuation and capture of Athens

At sea the Greeks had gained considerable confidence from their earlier successes and good luck, but a third day of fighting did not go so well for them. Their opponents had again managed to encircle them and in the ensuing struggle both sides suffered heavy casualties, which the Greeks could ill afford. After hearing the bad news from Thermopylai the Greek fleet headed for the island of Salamis, off the coast of Athens. They did this at the request of the Athenians, whose population was being evacuated to Troizen in the eastern

Peloponnese and the islands of Salamis and Aigina in an attempt to save them from the Persians. The decision to abandon Athens and Attika to the Persians and evacuate the population by sea was a brave one, made by a vote of the Athenian citizen assembly. It is a remarkable example of Athenian democracy in action, with the majority view prevailing after an impassioned debate, carried out under the shadow of the Persian invasion.

While the Persians were advancing through northern Greece the Athenians sent an official delegation to the famous oracle of the god Apollo at Delphi to ask for divine guidance. The usual procedure when consulting the oracle at Delphi was for the sacred envoys to the priestess of Apollo, called the Pythia, would then utter the god's words, which tended to be a stream of unintelligible phrases that the priests would have to 'interpret' for the suppliants. On this occasion, however, the envoys had scarcely taken their seats in the Pythia's sacred chamber before she screamed directly at them, saying, 'Wretched ones, why do you sit there? Leave your homes and your rocky citadel and flee to the ends of the earth!' This command was followed with dire warnings of impending doom not just for Athens, but for many other Greek cities at the hands of the Persians. Although they were taken aback by this outburst, the two Athenian envoys had a mission to complete, so they heeded the advice of a leading Delphic official and made another, humbler entreaty for Apollo's guidance. Their second approach yielded a somewhat more encouraging reply. As was usual, the oracle was delivered to the Athenians in poetic form:

It is not in the power of Pallas Athena to
appease Olympian Zeus, although she entreats
him with many words and subtle wisdom, but I
will speak a second time to you, having become
almost adamant.
When all the other places are seized that are
bounded by Kekrops and the secret groves of
divine Kithairon, heavenly Zeus gives to the

This Persian soldier is a member of the division known as the Immortals. There were 10,000 men in this division and it was always kept up to strength, making it seem as though none of its soldiers were ever killed. Unlike the heavily armoured Greek hoplites who specialised in fighting at close quarters, the Persian troops preferred to fight at a distance, relying on bows and arrows more than spears. (Ancient Art and Architecture)

to Athena being unable to appease Zeus, and the seizure of places within boundaries of Kekrops (a mythical king of Athens) and the groves of Mount Kithairon (on the border with Boiotia) suggested that the whole of Attika would be overrun by the Persians. The reference to a wooden wall remaining intact seemed to some Athenians to be a command to defend one area, logically the Acropolis of Athens, with a wooden palisade, but Themistokles and his supporters argued for another meaning. They pointed to the mention of Salamis, an island in the Saronic Gulf to the west of Athens, and the mention of an army coming from the mainland, interpreting the oracle as an instruction to abandon the overrun territory of Attika and retreat to Salamis. On their interpretation the wooden wall was a figurative one and meant the wooden hulls of the Athenians' new fleet of warships. The reference to Demeter, goddess of the harvest, even gave a time of year for the promised victory. Their arguments carried the day and the Assembly passed a decree ordering the evacuation and the preparation of the fleet. A revised version of this decree was preserved at Troizen. The following are extracts from it:

children of Triton a wooden wall that alone remains intact, to the benefit of you and your sons.

Do not wait for the army of cavalry and infantry coming from the mainland, but retreat and turn your backs on them. You shall confront them again.

Divine Salamis, you shall destroy the sons of women, either when Demeter is scattered or gathered together.

As often happened when states got an official response from the Delphic oracle, there was a dispute back in Athens over the significance of these words. The references

Decided by the Council and the People: Themistokles, the son of Neokles, of the deme Phrearrhioi proposed: The city is to be entrusted to the protection of its patron Athena and to the protection of all the other gods, against the barbarians on behalf of the land. The whole of the Athenians and the foreigners who live in Athens shall move their wives and children to Troizen ... and their old folk and moveable property to Salamis ... All the rest of the Athenians and the resident foreigners who have

reached manhood shall embark on the
200 ships prepared and fight against the
barbarians for the sake of their own freedom
and that of the other Greeks …

The decree was passed in the summer of
480, prior to the battle of Salamis. The
Athenians were committing themselves to
resisting the Persians and putting their
trust in the co-operation of the other
Greeks. An earlier decree had recalled all
those Athenian citizens who were ostracised
and required them to go to Salamis.
Several of Themistokles' political opponents
were among the exiles who assembled
there.

In the end a few people did remain
behind in the city, mainly the temple
treasurers and priestesses of the cults on the
Acropolis, which could not be abandoned
entirely to the enemy. Some of the poorer
Athenians persisted in the belief that a
literal wooden wall would be proof against
the Persians and they barricaded themselves
on the Acropolis behind a wooden palisade.
The Persians occupied Attika in early
September of 480 and ransacked Athens.
They took up a position on the Areopagos
hill, opposite the entrance to the Acropolis,
and fired flaming arrows into the palisade.
Some Athenians descended from Peisistratos
were with the Persians and they tried to
persuade the defenders to give in, but
eventually the Persians had to storm the
citadel. They killed the remaining defenders
then ransacked the temples and set fire
to them.

Xerxes also sent some of his army into
Phokis to ravage the countryside and loot
the towns. The Phokians fled westwards, as
did many of the citizens of Delphi, but the
sanctuary of Apollo escaped plundering by
the Persians. The story that Herodotus was
told to explain this, by the officials at
Delphi, held that as a Persian detachment
was approaching the remaining priests
asked the god what to do and he replied
that he would protect his own. Then, as
the Persian soldiers were coming up the
narrow mountain path to the sanctuary,

there was a crack of thunder and two
bolts of lightning struck the cliffs above
them, sending two enormous rocks crashing
down, killing some and putting the rest to
flight. An alternative explanation is that
Xerxes was well disposed towards the priests
at Delphi, who had done their best to
convince the Greeks that resistance was
futile, so he specifically exempted the
sanctuary from plunder. Respectful
treatment of this kind was not unusual
for major religious centres in the provinces
of the Persian Empire.

The fleets prepare to do battle

Having assisted in the evacuation of the
Athenians to Salamis the Greek fleet waited
in the bay on the east side of the island
while the commanders debated whether to
withdraw to the more defensible land
position at the Isthmus of Corinth. Many of
the Peloponnesian states had already
decided that this narrow strip of land
offered them the best chance of resisting the
Persian advance. When the news of the
defeat at Thermopylai reached them, the
Spartans and the other Peloponnesians, who
had just finished celebrating the Olympic
festival, immediately gathered at the
Isthmus and began constructing a
fortification wall across its narrowest point.
The fleet commanders began discussing
their options as the Persians were entering
Attika. After a day of inconclusive
arguments they broke up for the night.
The following day the Persian fleet arrived
and took up station in the waters beyond
the Bay of Phaleron to the east of Salamis.
Their numbers had been reduced by storms
and battle, but they had picked up some
reinforcements from Greeks who were
forced to come over to the Persian side, so
the effective strength was probably over
700 warships. The Greeks, who had only
just over 300 ships, did not come out to
fight. Instead they carried on with their
deliberations which were interrupted by the
news that the Persians had captured the

Acropolis. A large part of the Persian army also began to head for the Isthmus of Corinth. These developments only encouraged the majority of commanders to abandon Salamis before the Persian fleet closed in. Themistokles and the Athenians pleaded with Eurybiades, the Spartan who was still in overall command of the fleet, but he insisted that the Isthmus option was the best one. He ordered the ship's captains to prepare to depart under the cover of night. But later that night Eurybiades changed his mind and the following morning the Greek fleet was still at Salamis, ready to do battle with the Persians. What caused this change of plan?

Each fleet was aware of the other's position, although neither side had direct sight of their opponents and they were far enough apart to be able to carry out some manoeuvres undetected. The commanders needed to obtain further information before they made their next moves. From the Persians' point of view the information that mattered most was whether the Greek fleet was staying put at Salamis, or whether it was going to retreat westwards, via the Megarian Straits. To some extent this could be determined by observing the Greek position from the mainland opposite Salamis, although the small island of Hagios Georgios would have interfered with their view and, crucially, the Greeks could, if necessary, have slipped away under cover of darkness. From the Greek point of view the most important question was whether there was a realistic escape route available to them. The Persian army was moving along the coast of the Bay of Eleusis and would soon occupy the land immediately north of Salamis, as far as the Megarian Straits. If a section of the Persian fleet came around the south of Salamis and entered these straits from the west while the main fleet remained to the east, they would cut the Greeks off completely from the Peloponnese. A similar deployment had already been tried by the Persians against the Greeks when they were based at Artemision. But for the intervention of a

storm it might well have succeeded in trapping them on that occasion.

Herodotus says that this is precisely what the Persians did. He makes Themistokles responsible for prompting their deployment by saying that he sent a trusted slave, called Sikinnos, to Xerxes with a secret message, telling him that the Greeks were about to leave and urging him to seize his chance to attack them before they escaped. He claimed that Xerxes would catch them disunited and unprepared for battle and win an easy victory. Did Themistokles really send a message to the enemy and did they really believe that it was genuine? One reason for doubting the story is that Themistokles himself was later exiled by the Athenians and sought asylum with the Persians. His political enemies may have invented the message ploy to blacken his reputation. In any case, it is far from clear that the message would have made any difference. The Persians certainly began to move their ships into position that evening, but whether they did so on account of Themistokles' messenger, or because the king had independently decided to take the offensive that night is open to debate. They sent a squadron of 200 Egyptian ships round to the west side of Salamis to cut off the route to the Isthmus through the Megarian Straits. Another squadron was despatched with orders to cruise the southern and eastern approaches to the island while the rest of the fleet proceeded into the narrow straits between Salamis and the mainland towards the Greek positions. A small force of élite Persian infantry was landed on the tiny island of Psyttaleia to occupy it in anticipation of some ships being driven aground there during the fighting. It would have taken quite a long time for the Persian ships to move around from Phaleron to the opening of the straits, so even if they began to move at dusk, some of them may still have been taking up their stations towards midnight. Most of the captains were new to the waters around Salamis, and Herodotus adds the detail that these

movements were made 'silently', in order that the Greeks would be unaware of them. It seems reasonable to suppose that the Persians hoped to drive the Greeks out of the narrow channels around the eastern side of the island and into the more open waters of the Bay of Eleusis. The Greeks would not have been expected to attempt to defeat the main strength of Xerxes' navy, but rather to flee westwards and try to force their way past the smaller Egyptian detachment. Xerxes' commanders had to put his ships out to sea early, regardless of Themistokles' message, because he needed

The Hellenic Navy's vessel *Olympias* is a reconstruction of a trireme warship of the type used by the Athenians in the fifth century. The ship is rowed by up to 170 oarsmen, sitting in banks of three along each side. Triremes used sails to make voyages over long distances, but the sails and masts were normally left on shore for battles. Both Greeks and Persians used triremes as the standard vessel in their navies, but the greater resources of the Persian Empire meant that the Great King could afford to man larger fleets. (Ancient Art and Architecture)

ships they may have had at sea, might not have been able to see the Greeks if they decided to escape under cover of darkness, or even dusk. By closing off the possible escape routes as darkness fell they ensured that this could not happen.

The Greeks received two reports of these movements. One came from the crew of another Greek ship that defected from the Persians, this time from the island of Tenos. They revealed the Persian plan to Eurybiades and his commanders, but their reliability was questioned. Late in the evening, however, one of the returned Athenian exiles, Aristeides, came back from a scouting voyage with the news that the Persians were surrounding the Greek position and that retreating to the Isthmus was no longer possible without a fight. Themistokles renewed his urging to engage the Persian fleet, arguing that the narrows on the eastern side of Salamis would be a better place to fight them than the Bay of Eleusis, or the more open waters around the Isthmus. A threat made by Themistokles and his fellow Athenians to abandon the rest of the Greeks entirely and take their families away to Italy may have carried particular weight in the discussions. The Athenian ships made up by far the largest contingent in the Greek fleet, so their presence was essential in any naval confrontation with the Persians. Under the circumstances it is hardly surprising that Eurybiades changed his mind and agreed to lead the Greek fleet into battle. Any hope of slipping away under the cover of darkness had been dashed by the Persians deploying their ships ahead of the Greek

to close his trap before darkness fell and the Greeks could more easily escape. It is, therefore, not necessarily the case that Sikinnos' message prompted Xerxes to act. The Persians would have needed to follow the same timetable without it, since their observers on the mainland, plus any scout

departure. The only course of action left was to sail out to battle and trust that the Persian ships would be unable to use their numerical superiority in the relatively narrow waters.

The battle of Salamis

In eager anticipation of a magnificent victory, King Xerxes had an observation point prepared so that he could watch the battle. It was positioned opposite the town of Salamis with a good view of Psyttaleia, the island where a detachment of Persian troops had landed during the night. But instead of witnessing his fleet's final triumph over the Greeks, Xerxes saw a naval disaster unfolding before his very eyes. The various ethnic contingents of the Persian fleet were lined up several rows deep across the narrow channel between the Phoenicians on the right wing, nearest to Xerxes' position, and the Ionians on the left, nearest to Salamis. As they moved further into the channel their ships became so compacted and confused that they found it impossible to keep in formation. The crews had been up all night and were tired and to make matters worse a strong swell developed which made it even harder for the ships to make headway. Themistokles, who knew the local sea conditions very well, had anticipated this and he seems to have persuaded the other Greek commanders to delay engaging the Persians until they were clearly in disorder. This would explain the apparent retreat of the Greeks that Herodotus says preceded the first clash, and which can be interpreted as a change from a passive formation of ships in a line to a more active one, with the Athenian and Aiginetan ships on the two Greek wings leading the Greek charge to break through the Persian lines and ram individual ships as they struggled to manoeuvre. From the Persians' point of view, it would have appeared that the Greek ships were turning away, and they would obviously assume that they were trying to

retreat, which was what their own commanders had anticipated. The tragic playwright Aischylos, in his play *The Persians*, mentions a signal given to the Greek fleet by a trumpet, which may well have been a pre-arranged one to tell the captains when to move forward and strike. Signals had also been used to co-ordinate the actions of the Greek fleet at Artemision. It would seem, therefore, that both sides had to some extent determined in advance how the battle would be fought. Like all battles, however, once the action had started it would be impossible to keep to a specific plan, even if there was one, and it was up to the captains of the individual ships to make decisions on the spot. The main decision that many of Xerxes' captains made was to turn away from the attacking Greeks, causing more confusion as they encountered their own ships trying to go forward and impress the Great King with their prowess. In the resulting chaos the captains of the Greek ships urged on their much fresher crews and pressed the attack with great success.

Herodotus' subsequent account of the battle is largely made up of anecdotes about the exploits of various individuals and groups. These anecdotes, like so many of the stories Herodotus recounts throughout his *Histories*, are versions of events given to him by particular groups or individuals, so they are often very biased and we therefore do not have a complete picture of the battle. Herodotus repeats the story that, at the last minute, the 70 Corinthian ships did turn and flee towards the Bay of Eleusis. It is likely that this supposed cowardly, northward retreat, which Herodotus presents as an Athenian slander against the Corinthians, may have been a deliberate move to engage the Egyptian squadron and prevent it from attacking the Greeks at the rear. The Corinthians maintained that their ships did not encounter the Egyptians but returned to the battle and acquitted themselves as well as any of the other Greeks.

One of the most colourful anecdotes concerns Artemisia, the ruler of Halikarnassos, Herodotus' home city, which was subject to the Persians. She was in command of her own ship and in the front line of the Persian fleet. When an Athenian trireme bore down on her she tried to escape but found her path blocked by other Persian ships. In desperation she ordered her helmsman to ram one of them, a ship that was commanded by the king of Kalydna in Lykia. This ship sank with the loss of the king and all his crew. The pursuing Athenian captain assumed that Artemisia's ship was on his side and changed course towards another Persian vessel. Xerxes and his advisers saw the incident and recognised Artemisia's ship by its ensign, but they assumed that she had sunk a Greek trireme, which earned her the king's admiration. Xerxes is also said to have remarked at this point, 'My men have acted like women and my women like men.'

Another story concerns the Persian soldiers on the island of Psyttaleia. They were placed there in anticipation of the bulk of the Greek fleet being driven north and westwards away from the island. Instead they were isolated from their own ships and left vulnerable to attack from the nearby shores of Salamis. Aristeides, who had been elected as one of the Athenian generals after his early return from exile, commandeered some small boats and led a group of Athenian hoplites over to the island. Right before Xerxes' eyes, his élite troops, who included three of his own nephews, were slaughtered by the Athenians. Along the coast of Salamis other Persians who managed to get ashore from their foundering ships were killed or captured.

Some of the Phoenician ships, which had been closest to the king's position, encountered less trouble in advancing on the Greeks and joined in the battle sooner than the Ionians on the opposite wing. Their principal opponents were the Athenians, who routed them and drove several of the Phoenician crews ashore,

right at the place where Xerxes was watching from his royal chariot. They proceeded to the king and tried to excuse their failure by complaining that they had been betrayed by the Ionians, whom they blamed for the confusion in the Persian fleet. Unfortunately for them, while they were in the presence of the king, one of the Ionian ships, from Samothrake, was seen to ram an Athenian trireme and then get rammed by an Aiginetan one. The marines on the Ionian ship immediately boarded and captured the Aiginetan vessel, proving to Xerxes both their loyalty and their valour. The king was now so angry at what he was seeing that he gave orders for the Phoenician complainers to be beheaded.

Towards the end of the day the Persian fleet retreated in confusion to the Bay of Phaleron, having lost more than 200 ships and having failed in its objective of forcing the Greeks away from Salamis. The Greeks had lost only about 40 ships and had sent the enemy back to their anchorage in disarray. The unexpected victory naturally led many to interpret it as an act of divine power, a fulfilment of the Delphic oracle given to the Athenians earlier in the year. Stories quickly began to circulate about divine apparitions during the fighting, a mysterious flash of light seen coming from Demeter's sanctuary at Eleusis and the sound of a holy chorus chanting prayers. The story also grew that King Xerxes immediately abandoned his army and fled back to Asia.

In fact, although it was getting late in the year and the weather was increasingly unhelpful, Xerxes seems to have attempted to carry on with the campaign for several more days. He attempted to build another bridge of boats across the straits to Salamis and ordered his fleet to prepare for further action. The Persians still had far more ships than the Greeks and the Egyptian squadron must have rejoined the main fleet intact after it became clear that the Greeks were not going to be driven into their part of the trap. The army had marched through the

The battle of Salamis, 480

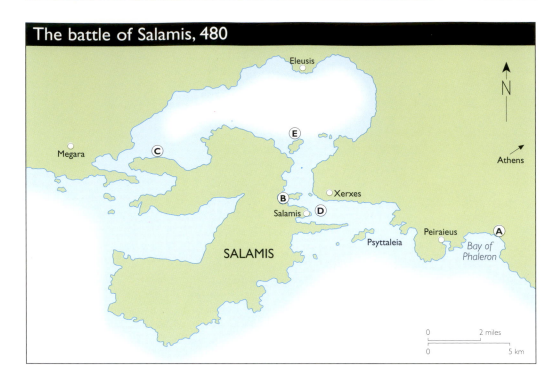

territory of Megara as far as the temple of Poseidon on the Isthmus, which was the headquarters of the Hellenic League. They ransacked and burned it, then moved up to, but did not challenge, the Greek defences further west. At this point Xerxes seems to have changed his mind and the Persian fleet departed for the shores of Asia Minor. The Greeks pursued them as far as Andros, but then gave up and returned to Salamis. Xerxes meanwhile took his army back through Boiotia and into Thessaly and Macedonia, where it could spend the winter in places with sufficient supplies of food and fodder. A portion of the army returned with the Great King himself to Persia.

The Greeks clearly thought that Xerxes had simply lost his nerve and run for home, but there were other reasons for his retreat and return to Persia. To some extent the campaign had been a success. While his fleet had not exactly covered itself with glory, his army had won the first major engagement, albeit with significant casualties. They had slain one of the principal enemy leaders and taken

ABOVE On the eve of the battle of the main Persian fleet left its station in the bay of Phaleron **(A)** and rowed quietly towards the position of the Greek fleet **(B)**. A detachment of 200 Egyptian ships was sent round the island of Salamis to the straits of Megara **(C)** to block off the route for a Greek retreat westwards. The Greeks rowed out at dawn and the main battle took place in the narrow channel **(D)** to the north of the tiny island of Psyttaleia, where Xerxes had stationed 400 elite troops. The Corinthian ships left the Greek fleet and sailed northwards towards the Egyptians, but after reaching approximately point **(E)** without coming into contact with the enemy they turned back and rejoined the main fleet. From his position on the headland opposite the town of Salamis Xerxes was able to see the entire battle.

RIGHT An archer wearing a Scythian-style pointed cap from the sculptures that decorated the temple at Aphaia on the island of Aigina. The Greeks used archers in warfare as support for their heavy infantrymen and in naval warfare. Archers were a standard part of the crews of triremes and were skilled at firing their bows from a kneeling or crouching stance to counteract the movement of the ship. (Ancient Art and Architecture)

possession of the city of the hated Athenians. Even after the move to Thessaly his empire had been substantially extended to the west and it might be argued that his presence was not essential to the rest of

the campaign, which could be resumed the following year. An eclipse of the sun occurred at the start of October. This may have been interpreted as an omen that Xerxes' patron god Ahuramazda was not favourably disposed towards further action for some time. There were also good political reasons for him not to stay out on the western extremities of his empire for too long, not least the danger of rebellion in some of the key satrapies. In 479 Xerxes suppressed another serious revolt in Babylonia and it is quite likely that news of the beginning of this unrest was what made him decide to leave Greece before the pacification of the new territories had been completed.

The battle of Plataia

The Persian commander left in Greece was Mardonios, a cousin of Xerxes and also his son-in-law; his second-in-command was Artabazos, who later became one of the satraps of Phrygia in western Asia Minor. Logistical requirements forced Mardonios to retire to Thessaly and Macedonia for the winter. His long-term objective was to crush the remaining Greek states and to do this he would clearly have to invade the Peloponnese. The defences at the Isthmus of Corinth were completed by early 479, making it a very strong position. It was necessary for Mardonios to prepare for the return of the Persian fleet, so in the spring of 479 he decided to try to break up the Hellenic League by inviting the Athenians to 'medise'. If he could remove their naval forces from the struggle, he would have a good chance of overcoming the remaining Greek ships and landing Persian troops behind the Isthmus defences. He used the king of Macedon, Alexander, to make the initial overtures because he was both a subject of the Great King and, partly as a result of supplying timber to build the Athenian fleet, he had been officially recognised as a friend and benefactor of the Athenian people. Mardonios offered to

get Xerxes' approval for the Athenians to retain their own territory, gain more at the expense of other Greeks and have their temples rebuilt at the king's expense.

On hearing of this development the Spartans hurriedly sent their own envoys to Athens to urge the Athenians not to leave the alliance. In spite of the attractions of Mardonios' offer the Athenians were resolute and insisted to Alexander that they would never make peace with Xerxes. At the same time they urged the Spartans to come out of the Peloponnese and fight to protect Attika, otherwise they might have to reconsider their position. This created a problem for the Spartans and the other Peloponnesian members of the Hellenic League, as there was no obvious place north of the Isthmus at which they could hope to bottle up the Persian army. They would have to risk a battle on more open ground against what was bound to be a larger army. The Spartans appointed Pausanias, a nephew of Leonidas, as regent for his young son, Pleistarchos, who was too young to command an army. Their other king, Leotychides, took command of the Hellenic fleet, which assembled at Aigina for the coming campaign.

In the summer Mardonios marched his army south, through Boiotia and towards Athens. Realising that help from the Peloponnese would not arrive in time, the Athenians staged another evacuation to Salamis. Mardonios refrained from ransacking Athens until the Athenians had been given another chance to accept his offer of peace. Herodotus says that when the offer was repeated to the Athenian council of 500, only one man suggested that it should be put to the citizen assembly for a vote, and he was stoned to death by his colleagues. They did send messengers to the Spartans to complain that they were being forced into a position where their only alternative was to join the Persians. This had the desired effect and a large army was assembled to challenge Mardonios. As well as several thousand *perioikoi* and thousands of other Peloponnesian hoplites, the army that marched with Pausanias out of the Peloponnese included 5,000 Spartan citizens, the largest Spartan force ever to do so.

From Mardonios' point of view the emergence of the Greeks from the Peloponnese was the next best thing to an Athenian defection. He moved his army to Thebes on the plains of Boiotia, which were flat enough for him to exploit his advantages in numbers and make good use of his cavalry. Pausanias was joined by a large Athenian force as well as several other groups of allies. The Greek army eventually settled into a strong position on the northern slopes of Mount Kithairon, facing the Persians, who established a fortified camp across the river Asopos on the open plain, which was more suited to their cavalry. The Spartans and Tegeans were on the right of the line, the rest of the Peloponnesians in the centre and the Athenians and Megarians on the left. The total number of Greek hoplites according to Herodotus was 38,700, more than four times as many as fought at Thermopylai. There were also tens of thousands of helots accompanying the Spartans and many light infantrymen from the other Greek states.

Mardonios probably had many more men than Pausanias, including several thousand soldiers from Thebes and the other Boiotian cities, although not the Plataians who fought on the Greek side. His army contained a lot more cavalry than the Greeks' and he used it to harass the supply lines of Pausanias and his men. On one occasion his cavalry captured a whole Greek supply column. They also succeeded in rendering unusable the main source of drinking water for the Greeks, a spring called Gargaphia. These cavalry raids continued for nearly two weeks, gradually reducing the Greek supply lines until Pausanias was left with no choice but to move his army closer to the city of Plataia, where there was water and a good supply of food.

Pausanias decided on a night-time withdrawal and sent messages to the various contingents of his army to retire under cover of darkness. The left wing of the Greek army retreated almost to the walls of Plataia, but there was confusion among some of the Spartan and Peloponnesian contingents. According to one story that Herodotus was told, a Spartan commander flatly refused to retreat and this delayed the movement of the rest, so they were still a long way from their destination when dawn broke and the Persian cavalry renewed their attacks. Mardonios was informed by his scouts that the Greeks were in retreat and he decided to attack them while they were not properly formed up for battle. Mardonios' Persian infantry engaged the Spartans and the Tegeans, who were nearest to them, while Pausanias sent a messenger to summon the rest of his army to his aid, but they were prevented from doing so by the Boiotians and other Greeks in Mardonios' army, who hurried across the river Asopos to attack the former left wing of Pausanias' army, including the Athenians. The Spartans and Tegeans had to fight Mardonios' main force on their own. The odds were against them, but the Greeks were better equipped for close-quarter combat and the Spartans excelled in disciplined fighting as a unit. After a hard struggle the Greeks forced their opponents back and Mardonios himself was killed. This caused a general panic in the Persian lines as men rushed back to the sanctuary of their camp. On the other side of the battlefield the hoplites from Athens, Phleious and Megara were initially harassed by Boiotian and Thessalian cavalry, but eventually closed with the main body of Theban infantry and overcame them, putting the Thebans to flight as well. The Tegeans and Spartans were temporarily unable to storm the Persian camp, which was protected by a strong stockade, but the arrival of the Athenians enabled them to storm the defences and capture substantial amounts of booty, as well as many prisoners.

Without waiting to recover any bodies, even that of Mardonios, Artabazos withdrew with what remained of the Persian army, still perhaps as many as 40,000. He marched straight out of Greece and back to Asia Minor. The Greek casualties were astonishingly light, amounting to only 91 Spartans, 16 Tegeans and 52 Athenians, although the Megarians and Phleiasians suffered badly at the hands of the Boiotian cavalry, leaving 600 dead on the plain. This resounding Hellenic League victory ended the Persian threat to the mainland of Greece. Eleven days after the battle the victorious Greeks marched on Thebes, the Greek city that had been a major base for the Persians after Thermopylai and which had contributed strongly to Mardonios' army. The Athenians were particularly keen to see their Boiotian neighbours made to pay for deserting the Hellenic cause. After a siege of 20 days the Thebans surrendered, offering up those of their leading citizens whom they judged were most to blame for their collaboration with the Persians. Pausanias disbanded his army, took the Theban prisoners to Corinth and executed them.

Pausanias was treated as the hero of the hour. He was awarded a tenth of all the booty from the Persian camp, which included many gold and silver items as well as expensive tents and other equipment for the Persian nobility. There were many non-combatants among the prisoners, including servants, concubines and other attendants. Pausanias had Mardonios' cooks prepare a typical Persian banquet in their master's richly decorated tent. Alongside this he had a standard Spartan meal displayed for comparison. With dry humour he remarked to the other commanders that it showed the folly of the Persians, who had so much luxury at their disposal but who still tried to plunder the poor Greeks. To commemorate their victory the states of the Hellenic League dedicated a golden tripod to Apollo at Delphi. It stood on a bronze column carved in the form of three

PHASE ONE Pausanias' army initially occupied the small ridge above the Asopos river, to the north east of Plataia and used the Gargaphia spring for water. Persian and allied Greek cavalry cut off their supply route from Plataia and rendered the spring unusable, so Pausanias ordered a retreat at night towards Plataia. At dawn his left wing (the Athenians and Megarians) was close to Plataia, with his centre (made up of Peloponnesians) alongside, but the right wing (Spartans, Perioikoi and Tegeans) were delayed. When the Persian cavalry made contact with the Spartans Mardonios ordered his whole army across the river Asopos to attack the Greeks.

PHASE TWO The Spartans and Tegeans defeated the Persians opposing them, killed Mardonios and drove his men back to the Persian camp. They were followed by the other Peloponnesians. The Athenians and Megarians were initially prevented from linking up with them by the Boiotians and other Greeks fighting on the Persian side. A total of 600 Megarians were killed as they crossed the plain towards the Spartans. Eventually the Athenians drove their opponents away and joined in the assault on the Persian camp.

intertwined snakes, emblems of Apollo. In the fourth century AD, Constantine took this monument to decorate the hippodrome of his new city of Constantinople. The lower parts of the snakes can still be seen there today. The Spartans had the names of the Greek states whose men fought against the Persians carved onto the coils of the snakes, but Pausanias put his own name on the base, claiming that it was his right to do so as principal commander of the Greeks.

The battle of Mykale

The defeat of Xerxes' fleet at Salamis encouraged some of the cities of the northern Aegean to rebel against the Persians. Among these the most important were Olynthos and Poteidaia. They were both besieged by the army of Artabazos, who had taken 60,000 men through Macedonia and Thrace to escort Xerxes back to Asia Minor. Olynthos fell to a determined assault and its population was massacred to discourage further revolts. Poteidaia was less easy to attack and Artabazos spent three months besieging it

The battle of Plataia, 479: Phase one

The battle of Plataia, 479: Phase two

before he had to give up and rejoin Mardonios. Nevertheless the Greeks felt that there was a strong likelihood of detaching more of their Ionian brethren from the Persians, so they sailed to Samos where Xerxes' fleet had been stationed for the winter, with a small army nearby, so that it could keep a watch on the Ionian Greeks.

The Greek fleet was much smaller than that which fought at Salamis, mainly because so many men were committed to the defence of the mainland. Herodotus says that only 110 ships gathered at Aigina in the spring under the command of the Spartan king, Leotychides. Themistokles was not as popular among the Athenians as he had hoped, probably because so many of them had lost their homes and property when the Persians sacked Athens, so he did not lead the small Athenian contingent, which was commanded by one of his rivals, Xanthippos. After the disaster of Salamis, however, the Persian commander, Tigranes, another cousin of Xerxes, was clearly unwilling to face the Greeks in a sea battle and he sent the best ships, from Phoenicia,

back to their home ports and disembarked the crews of the rest on the mainland promontory of Mykale, opposite Samos. They fortified their encampment and awaited the enemy. Leothychides also disembarked his crews and led the Greek soldiers against the Persian positions. As he approached the Persians he invited the Ionians among them to defect, which led the Persians to disarm the Samians, whose possession of a large island home might have made them more inclined to defy the Great King than those who dwelt on the mainland. Indeed, the paths leading over the mountain and away from the main Persian fortifications, which provided a possible escape route, were guarded by Greeks from Miletos, whose loyalty was not in question.

OVERLEAF This red-figure painted jug from Athens illustrates an artistic theme that was very popular in the fifth century. It shows a figure wearing Median dress of a patterned tunic and trousers and riding a horse. The rider is presented as one of the Amazons, a mythical tribe of women warriors, but the image symbolises the might of the Persians. (Ancient Art and Architecture)

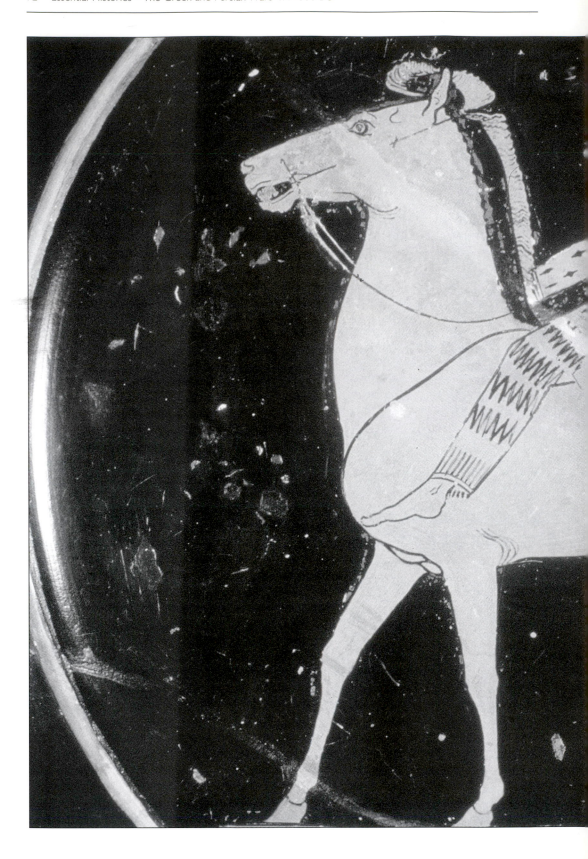

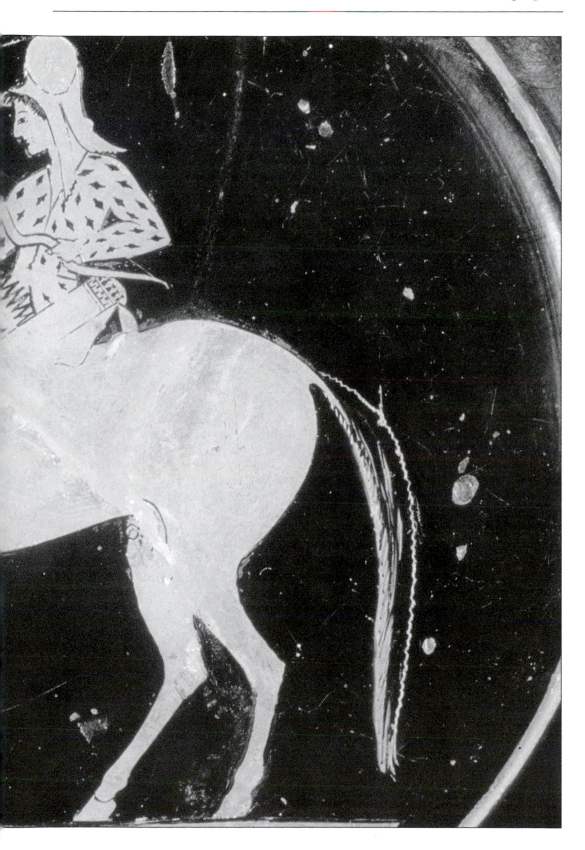

Leotychides and his men approached the Persian camp from the east and launched an attack. After prolonged fighting outside the camp the Persians retreated behind the stockade, which was soon breached, with some help from the Samians who were being held inside. Many of the Persians took their prepared escape route and eventually reached the satrapal capital of Sardis, but their commander Tigranes was killed. This victory on enemy territory encouraged wider rebellion among the Ionians and created something of a dilemma for the Hellenic League. How could they protect the rebel Ionians at such a distance and under the very noses of the Persian satraps? The Peloponnesians proposed transporting the Ionians back to Greece and giving them the cities of those Greeks who had medised. The Athenians objected strongly to this and eventually Leotychides was forced to admit those of them who were islanders, including the people of Samos, Lesbos and Chios into the League. They then sailed to the Hellespont, with the idea of destroying Xerxes' bridges, but they had already been broken up by a storm. Leotychides and the Peloponnesians sailed home, but Xanthippos and the Athenians remained in the Hellespont and took the city of Sestos after a siege. In the minds of the Athenians the emphasis was now shifting from defending Greece to making war on the territory of the Persian king.

Aristodemos the Spartan

One of the many individuals whom we encounter in the course of Herodotus' *Histories* is the Spartan citizen Aristodemos, who died at the battle of Plataia. From the details that Herodotus provides and from other sources of information we can trace his life and gain some revealing insights into the Spartan character. Aristodemos was born to a Spartan couple in one of the five villages that comprised the 'city' of Sparta, probably some time between 520 and 515. He was named after the mythical father of the first two Spartan kings. A Spartan father did not automatically have the right to raise his own sons. As soon as they were born he was obliged to show them to a group of older citizens who would inspect the infant and decide whether he was physically normal and likely to be a healthy child. Any children who failed this inspection were placed in an isolated gorge on Mount Taygetos and left to die. The boys who passed the inspection were deliberately toughened from an early age, by bathing them in wine, feeding them with plain food and getting them accustomed to enduring harsh conditions. On reaching the age of five, a boy was removed from his parental home and placed with other boys of the same age in a barracks. He stayed in this group until he reached manhood, around the age of 19 or 20, and was admitted to the ranks of Spartan citizens as one of the Equals.

Aristodemos' upbringing

The upbringing of Spartan boys was organised as a formal training called the *agoge*, aimed at preparing them for their future role as citizen soldiers. It therefore concentrated on skills and attributes thought appropriate to a hoplite. Discipline, conformity and group values were emphasised, as were physical and mental toughness. Singing and dancing were compulsory, with a focus on keeping in time and learning to recite by heart the choral poems of Tyrtaios. From the age of 10 athletic training, singing and dancing were also competitive, with regular prizes for the best boys and tests to determine if they were strong enough to proceed from one stage to the next.

The young boys went barefoot and wore very little clothing, being allowed only a single cloak for protection against the weather. They often exercised naked, as did the Spartan girls, who were not put through the *agoge*, but were raised to be fit and tough, so that they would produce strong healthy children. Food was simple and scarce, both to encourage a slim physique and to accustom the boys to function properly while hungry. This also encouraged them to steal additional food, which was not disapproved of, because it promoted stealth and resourcefulness, but they were severely punished if they were so careless as to be caught. A famous story was told of the Spartan boy who was caught by one of his elders and tried to hide a fox that he was carrying in his cloak. The fox gnawed through his stomach, but the boy did not cry out for fear of revealing it, so he died rather than be discovered. All stages of the *agoge* were supervised by older men, some of whom became close friends of individual boys. This practice often led to pederasty, but it was encouraged as a way of integrating the boys with the older men whom they would eventually join on a permanent basis as members of a *syssition*, or citizens' barracks.

The duties of a Spartan

Aristodemos passed all the tests and was elected to one of the *syssitia*. He was now a full Spartan citizen and had to be ready to be called up into action as part of a Spartan army, which usually comprised men aged between 20 and 40. When he reached his mid-20s he was required to take a wife. His choice of partner would to some extent have been his own, but it may have required the approval of the senior men of his village, and the girl's father would have had to approve of him as a husband. Men normally married women five or so years younger than them. The purpose of marriage was to produce more children for the Spartan state, so that the numbers of Spartans were maintained. A close emotional bond between husband and wife was not considered necessary. Until the age of 30 Aristodemos did not live with his wife, but stayed in the barracks with his *syssition* comrades. His visits to his wife were supposed to be carried out only in darkness and not too frequently. They were, however, expected to result in pregnancy. If they did not, he would not have been expected to keep his wife, but to repudiate her as barren and find another. Aristodemos did father at least one child, a son, and may have had more.

Once he turned 30 Aristodemos was considered a full Spartan citizen. He could now live in a house with his wife and family. He would join in the supervision of boys and young men and train with his messmates for war. The older Spartans were expected to be role models for the younger ones, examples of *andragathia*, meaning 'manly virtue'. A fine opportunity for Aristodemos to put his training into practice and demonstrate his manliness arrived in 480 when he marched off to face the Persians at Thermopylai. Aristodemos would normally have expected to go to war with the other mature men of his village, grouped in a regiment of up to 1,000 men, which was called a *lochos*. For Thermopylai special arrangements were made, because there was an important religious festival going on and it was considered insulting to the gods for the Spartan army to leave before it was completed. King Leonidas was chosen to command the Greek army and he obtained a

special religious dispensation to take 300 men, as a bodyguard. He would normally have been assigned young men in their 20s, but in view of the likelihood that they might be defeated by the huge Persian army he decided to choose older men, who had already produced at least one son to maintain the ranks of the Spartans. Aristodemos was among those chosen and doubtless considered it a great honour to be singled out in this way.

Aristodemos at Thermopylai

At the pass of Thermopylai, while the Greeks were waiting for the Persians to make their move they had plenty of time to contemplate the enormous size of Xerxes' army. It was probably at this time that one of the local Trachinian men remarked that when the Persians finally got round to shooting off their arrows there would be so many of them that they would blot out the sun. One of the Spartans, called Dienekes, said to his comrades, 'What our friend from Trachis says is good news, for if the Medes hide the sun then we shall be fighting in the shade.' It is also likely that, as they waited, the Spartans recited some of the more inspiring of Tyrtaios' verses. King Leonidas is said to have particularly approved of Tyrtaios' poems as suitable for firing up the spirits of the younger men so that they would be brave and daring in battle. The following extract from fragment 12 shows clearly how Tyrtaios emphasised the hoplite virtues of bravery, standing firmly together and being ready to sacrifice one's life for the sake of others:

No man has high regard in war unless he is able to stomach the sight of blood and death, and fight the enemy at close quarters.

This is excellence, the best prize that men who are young and bold can win.

It does all the people of the state good whenever a man stands firm in the front ranks, holding his ground and steadfastly refusing to even think of shameful flight, risking his life with a stout heart and shouting encouragement to those around him.

Such a man has high regard in war.

He speedily forces back the ranks of enemy spears and his eagerness turns the battle's tide.

He who loses his life falling in the front ranks, brings glory to his father, his comrades and his city, his chest, his armour and his bossed shield pierced many times by blows from the front.

Young and old mourn him alike and the whole state is saddened by his loss.

His tomb and his children get pointed out as do his children's children and all his line.

Never do the name and glory of his bravery die out, but he is immortal even as he lies in his grave, whichever man the war god Ares slays as he fights for his homeland and his children, standing firmly and bravely.

This fragment describes more or less what happened to the Spartans with Leonidas at the pass of Thermopylai; all, that is, except for two. Aristodemos and another Spartan called Eurytos had picked up eye infections which became so acute that they were told by the king to remove themselves from the ranks of the 300 as they were incapable of fighting. They were taken to the nearby village of Alpenos by their helot attendants to recuperate. As the majority of the Greek army retreated past them, sent away by Leonidas before the Persians could surround them, the two Spartans argued over whether it was their duty to go back and die with their comrades, even though they could not see, or stay out of the battle as ordered. Eventually Eurytos forced his helot to lead him back to the battle and was promptly slain, though the helot managed to escape. Aristodemos obeyed orders and stayed put, thereby surviving the battle. One other Spartan, called Pantites, also survived because he had been sent off to Thessaly as a messenger before the battle started and by the time he got back it was over.

The 'trembler'

While Leonidas and his 298 dead Spartans were praised as great heroes, Aristodemos and Pantites found themselves despised

when they got back to Sparta. It was generally felt that if they were true Spartans they would have died with their comrades. They were assumed to have been too afraid to fight, a slur on his manly virtue that Aristodemos felt very strongly. His sense of hurt would only have been compounded by the epitaph which was composed for the Spartans who died with Leonidas at Thermopylai. It was inscribed on a monument erected at the place where they made their final stand:

Stranger, tell the Spartans that we lie here in obedience to their words.

Yet Aristodemos had been ordered by Leonidas to retire from the battlefield and he obeyed the king's orders. It was only the difference of opinion with Eurytos, who had disobeyed his orders and returned to Thermopylai, that had caused the other Spartans to criticise Aristodemos for not doing likewise. Some people even suggested that he and Pantites had both been sent as messengers and had deliberately delayed their return to avoid the battle. In short they were both labelled cowards. The accusation of being a coward was the most damning that could be made against a true Spartan. Men who had run away from the enemy or refused to fight alongside their comrades were called *tresantes* meaning 'tremblers'. They were despised because they were the very opposite of the Spartan hoplite ideal. 'Tremblers' were required to wear coloured patches on their red cloaks to distinguish them and they were shunned by the rest of the Equals. Their own messmates from the *syssition* would have nothing to do with them, even to the point of refusing to speak to them. They could not hold any of the public offices and were unable to gain justice for insults or injuries, nor could they make legal agreements with other Spartans. No Spartan would allow his daughter to marry a 'trembler' and Aristodemos must have been concerned for the future of his own offspring, for no one would want to marry their children to the sons or daughters of a

This modern statue of the Spartan king, Leonidas, stands in the centre of the town of Sparta. Inscribed below is a famous two-word reply he is said to have given when the Spartans were invited by Xerxes at the battle of Thermopylai to surrender by laying down their arms. Leonidas answered him in Greek, 'Molon labe,' meaning, 'Come and take them.' (Ancient Art and Architecture)

'trembler'. Pantites found it all too much to bear and hanged himself, but Aristodemos endured the shame, hoping for an opportunity to restore his reputation.

Aristodemos at Plataia

That opportunity came the following year. In spite of the accusations of cowardice and his isolation from the rest of the Equals, Aristodemos was among those men who were called up by the ephors the following year to join the army that the regent Pausanias took to the battle of Plataia. The Spartans were anxious to have as large an army as possible so they probably sent almost all the citizens aged under 40, keeping only the oldest men back to guard Sparta against a possible Messenian helot uprising. Aristodemos marched with the men of his *lochos*, but he will still have been cold-shouldered by them. His only company would have been his personal helot attendant, carrying his equipment and cooking for him. As he approached the plain of Boiotia where the Persians were camped, his one aim will have been to show that he was not a coward, but a true Spartan. By an act of conspicuous bravery he could earn public honour and restore his reputation, even if it should cost him his life it would be worth it for the sake of his family.

Pausanias positioned his army on a ridge of hills near Plataia, but several days of cavalry attacks forced him to retreat by night. The Persians attacked the Spartans at dawn, first with cavalry and then infantry, who halted within bowshot of the Spartans and fired arrows at them from behind a wall of wicker shields. Pausanias needed to charge the Persians, but he delayed, waiting for reinforcements and good omens. It was usual for the commander, accompanied by the two ephors and his official diviners, to sacrifice a goat just before the ranks of the Spartan charged forward to engage with the enemy and to inspect its entrails to see if the gods were sending a good omen for the success of the battle. When the ephors and the diviners pronounced the omens favourable then the army could charge. The first time that Pausanias did this the omens were unfavourable, so he ordered the Spartans to wait. The men grew increasingly impatient as the Persians poured more arrows into their ranks, so Pausanias sacrificed again, and again, but still he did not give the order to charge. Eventually Aristodemos could take no more and, without waiting for the command, he broke out of the ranks of his *lochos* and charged at the Persians. To his left the Tegeans also rushed forward. Pausanias chose this moment to order the Spartans forward as well, as apparently the omens were now good. Aristodemos probably killed several Persians before he was cut down himself. The Spartans and Tegeans drove the Persians back, killed their commander Mardonios and won the battle.

Aristodemos certainly showed courage with his charge at the Persian ranks, and Herodotus felt that he was the bravest man on that day, but the Spartans did not agree. They refused to honour him as a hero of the state because they felt he had deliberately chosen to get himself killed. He had shown that he had the courage of a true Spartan, but he had failed to meet their high standards of discipline and obedience. Although he did not have his tomb and his children pointed out to later generations, nevertheless, thanks to the enquiries of Herodotus, he has achieved lasting fame.

Persian architecture

The Persians in Athenian tragedy

Twice each year the Athenians gathered in the theatre of Dionysos to watch and listen to choral competitions. By the early fifth century the format of these performances had evolved into dramatic plays, with carefully written scripts exploring tragic or comic themes. Some of the best examples have been preserved and they still have the power to enthral audiences nearly two and a half thousand years after their original performances. The tragic plays usually took their storylines from the rich traditions of Greek mythology, but occasionally a playwright would give his work a contemporary setting.

In 493 the Athenian tragedian Phrynikos presented a play entitled *The Capture of Miletos* in the theatre of Dionysos at Athens. The play, which took as its theme the recent fall of this great Ionian city to the Persians and the murder or enslavement of many of its people, was so moving that the audience was reduced to tears. This highly emotional reaction prompted the Athenians to fine Phrynikos and pass a decree that his play should never be performed again. The Athenians recognised that the fate of Miletos might be theirs if they resisted the Persians. Herodotus says that they fined Phrynikos because he reminded them of their own misfortunes and the looming threat of the Persian Empire. The text of the play has not been preserved.

In 472, however, eight years after the battle of Salamis, the great tragedian Aischylos, who had fought at Salamis and whose brother, Kynegeiros, had been killed in the battle of Marathon, produced a more popular play entitled *The Persians*. It was a great triumph for Aischylos and won first prize in the competition. The *choregos*, whose civic duty it was to pay for the production was Pericles, the son of the Athenian general, Xanthippos. The text of this play allows us to see part of the process by which the significance of the Persian Wars was defined for later generations. The dramatic action of the play takes place in the palace of the Persian king, Xerxes, where his courtiers and family are waiting for news of his expedition to conquer the Greeks. Through accounts of his actions Xerxes is characterised as an impetuous and dictatorial man whose pride and ambition will lead the Persians to disaster. This is a typical scenario for an Athenian tragedy, but the play is unique among the surviving examples of such works in its use of a contemporary subject and its presentation of the story from the perspective of the Persian court.

In the following extract (lines 230–45) Atossa, widow of King Dareios and mother of King Xerxes, is asking the Chorus, made up of elderly Persian men, to tell her more about the destination of her son's expedition, for she has had a dream that forebodes disaster. Shortly afterwards a messenger arrives with news of her son's defeat at Salamis.

Atossa: *This is something I want to learn my friends: where on the earth is Athens situated?*

Chorus: *Far away, as far as the point where the sun sets.*

Atossa: *Is this the city that my son is so keen to destroy?*

Chorus: *Yes, for so shall he make all of Greece subject to the king.*

Atossa: *Have they then so many men in their armies?*

Chorus: *Yes their army was strong enough to do the Medes great harm.*

Atossa: *What else is there about them? Are they a very wealthy city?*

The remains of the *Apadana* or audience hall of the royal palace at Persepolis. There were originally 72 limestone columns like these, rising to a height of over 20 metres. They supported the massive roof beams of cedar, brought from Lebanon. The *Apadana* was open on three sides to allow light to get in and to provide the king with viewing points to watch ceremonies and processions in the courtyards of the palace. (Ancient Art and Architecture)

Chorus: *They have a spring of silver, the earth's treasury.*
Atossa: *Do they arm themselves with bows and arrows?*
Chorus: *Not at all; they fight close with spears and carry shields.*
Atossa: *Who is their leader, the commander of their army?*
Chorus: *Of no man are they the slaves or the subjects.*
Atossa: *How then can they withstand an enemy's onslaught?*
Chorus: *Well enough to have destroyed the magnificent army of Dareios.*
Atossa: *What you say is terrible news for the parents of our men.*

This brief exchange shows that the Athenians saw themselves as the liberators of the Greeks through the bravery of their hoplites, at Marathon, and the skills of the navy, which they built from the profits of their silver mines, at Salamis. They also thought of themselves as superior to the Persians because they were not 'slaves' to a single ruler. This view that the Greek victories in the Persian Wars were a triumph of Athenian democracy and liberty over Persian monarchy and slavery disguises the fact that the Athenians had many allies whose regimes were far from democratic and that they themselves were happy to make other Greeks their subjects. Nevertheless it was a powerful idea and has continued to inform all subsequent discussions of the wider significance of the Persian Wars.

Persepolis, pinnacle of Persian royal architecture

The Greeks were astounded that they had managed to defeat the army and navies of the Great King of Persia. They were used to the idea that the Persians were fabulously wealthy and powerful and that the sheer size of their empire made them invincible. To a considerable extent this was an image that the Persian kings had deliberately fostered. In the Near-Eastern world of the fifth century there was nowhere that seemed as far away and yet so impressive as the Persian capital of Persepolis. For most people it took many months of travelling to reach it, at the heart of the Persian Empire, and few ever got to see it, but Persepolis represented the pinnacle of Achaemenid imperial architecture.

The king who started the building at Persepolis was Dareios. He wanted to have a new capital for the new dynasty that he had created. His work was continued by his son Xerxes and finished by Xerxes' son Artaxerxes. It was a monumental example of how effective the Persian kings were at utilising the resources of their vast empire. They took materials and craftsmen from all corners of the empire, even some Ionian Greeks are recorded among the craftsmen who built the palaces, and the numerous workers. The palaces were built to be impressive and to give visitors a sense of the overwhelming power and majesty of the Persian kings. Even as ruins they still convey that sense of power today.

Demokedes and Demaratos

Demokedes, a royal doctor

There are several stories in Herodotus' account of the Persian Wars of Greek exiles who had ended up living in Persia but who looked for an opportunity to return to their homeland. One of the most unusual ones concerns the doctor Demokedes, son of Kalliphon. He was a native of the Greek city of Kroton, in southern Italy, where a renowned school of medicine was developing. According to Herodotus, after learning the basics of the medical profession, as far as it was known at that time in Kroton, Demokedes quarrelled with his father and decided to leave Italy in 526 and try to make his fortune. He set himself up in Aigina, where he specialised in a form of medicine that, unlike the prevalent medical practices of the time, did not rely upon surgical instruments to cut and probe; he may have preferred the use of manipulation, massage and lotions. So successful were his techniques that after only a year Demokedes was being paid a retainer of 6,000 drachmas by the people of Aigina. The following year he was lured to Athens by Hippias, the son of Peisistratos, who paid him 10,000 drachmas, and the next year Polykrates, the tyrant of Samos, paid him 12,000 drachmas to come and practise there.

While he was in Samos Polykrates was captured and killed by the Persian satrap Oroites, who made slaves of the men of Polykrates' household, including Demokedes. Oroites was himself killed on the orders of King Dareios, who seems to have seen the ambitious satrap as a threat to his own position, and his slaves became the property of the king. Some time later Dareios dislocated his ankle when getting off his horse and the royal physicians, who were mostly Egyptians, were unable to heal the injury. In desperation, Dareios, in great pain and incapacitated by the injury, agreed to be treated by the Greek slave, whom one of his advisers remembered from his earlier days as the court physician to Polykrates. Demokedes reset the ankle and the king recovered completely, whereupon he installed Demokedes in his household and instructed all of his wives to reward him with gold for saving the king's life. He also cured the principal wife, Atossa, a daughter of Kyros the Great, of an abscess on her breast.

Demokedes could presumably have lived out his days as a respected member of the Persian king's retinue. He would have been housed and fed at royal expense, with allocations of grain, wine and other necessities provided for him from the royal storehouses. When Dareios was planning to extend his empire westwards, however, as a reward for curing queen Atossa, Demokedes contrived to be included in a reconnaissance expedition comprising 15 Persian nobles whom Dareios sent with two triremes and a supply ship to study the coasts and harbours of Greece and Italy. Having finished their survey of Greece the Persians proceeded to the city of Taranto in southern Italy, where Demokedes escaped from their supervision by telling the authorities that they were royal spies. From Taranto he made his way back to Kroton, where the Persians followed him and tried to apprehend him as a 'runaway slave of the king', but were resisted by the people of Kroton. The Persians eventually made their way back to Dareios, but only after being shipwrecked in the Straits of Otranto.

Demokedes' tale is typical of the oral sagas that Herodotus collected on his travels around the Mediterranean and the Near East. The basic outline may be reliable, although we cannot be certain about any of it, as no other records of Demokedes have survived. A renowned physician might indeed have moved from one Greek city to another and ended up working for the Persian king, who could afford to be far more generous than anyone else. Yet it is clear that many of the details that Herodotus was told are highly suspect. He claims that Demokedes at first pretended to Dareios that he was not a physician and had to be threatened with torture in order to admit to some medical knowledge, yet Dareios immediately surrendered himself to his care. Queen Atossa is supposed to have suggested the reconnaissance expedition to Dareios in their bedroom simply as a favour to Demokedes, who wanted to get back home. These embellishments make the story more entertaining, but they also provide ammunition for those who prefer to see Herodotus not as the Father of History, but as the Father of Lies.

Demaratos, a Spartan king in exile

Even a Spartan could find himself serving the Persian king. We first encounter the Spartan king Demaratos in Herodotus' account of what happened when a large Peloponnesian force invaded Attika in 506, led by both of the kings. The aim of the expedition was to overthrow the newly created democratic regime of Kleisthenes and to restore his defeated opponent Isagoras to power. Demaratos was persuaded by some of his allies, especially the Corinthians, that they were not justified in trying to force the Athenians to take back an exiled aristocrat and dismantle a regime that had come to power with popular support. Demaratos backed the Corinthian decision to pull out of the invasion, which had to be called off. As a

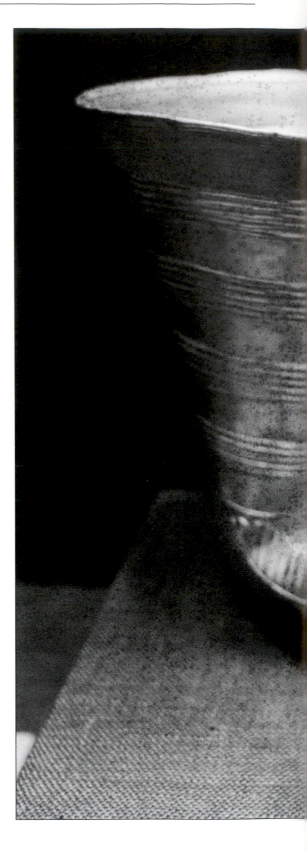

A golden *rhyton* or drinking vessel with its handle carved into the shape of a winged lion. The Achaemenid kings and the Persian aristocrats who accompanied them on their military expeditions took with them a large amount of gold and silver items such as these. When the Greeks captured Persian camps at the battles of Marathon and Plataia they were amazed at the wealth and luxury enjoyed by the barbarians. (Ancient Art and Architecture)

result of this disagreement between the two kings the Spartans decided that there should be no more jointly led expeditions, but that one king should always remain at Sparta.

The incident also sparked off a long-term feud between the two kings. Demaratos brought charges of corruption against the other king, Kleomenes, over the invasion of Attika and Kleomenes responded by plotting with Demaratos' cousin, Leotychides, to depose Demaratos. The grounds for this were, they claimed, that Demaratos was not the legitimate son of his predecessor, Ariston. There was some doubt over the matter because Demaratos' mother, who had been Ariston's third wife, gave birth prematurely and Ariston was thought to have had suspicions about the child's paternity. Eventually, in 491, rumours circulated by Kleomenes and Leotychides forced the ephors to act. As they usually did in moments of crisis the Spartan magistrates consulted the oracle of Apollo at Delphi. Kleomenes bribed the priests at Delphi to issue a false oracle saying that Demaratos was illegitimate. Consequently the ephors deposed Demaratos and made his cousin king in his place. Demaratos was briefly kept on at Sparta as a magistrate, but Leotychides forced him to leave Sparta. He sought refuge with the Persian king, Dareios, who gave him lands and made him a member of his court. He probably did this because he was about to invade Greece and wanted to use disaffected Greek aristocrats as governors of the newly conquered territories. Hippias, the former tyrant of Athens, was also among Dareios' courtiers. He went with the expedition of 490 but after the defeat at Marathon his chances of being reinstated as ruler of Athens disappeared and he died soon afterwards.

The grave monument of an Athenian citizen hoplite called Ariston. He wears a small bronze helmet and a cuirass made of toughened leather and linen, with a tunic beneath. He also has bronze greaves to protect his lower legs. His only weapon is a long spear. It was men like this who defied the army of the Spartan king, Kleomenes, that sought to prevent Kleisthenes' democratic reforms from being implemented in 507. (Ancient Art and Architecture)

According to Herodotus, Demaratos was ordered to accompany Dareios' son Xerxes on his invasion of Greece in 480. It is likely that Xerxes had promised to get him restored to his position in Sparta, as a subject ruler under the authority of the Persian king. Herodotus says that Xerxes consulted Demaratos several times about the strength and character of the Spartans. On the first occasion, after the crossing of the Hellespont, Demaratos, who had got used to the politics of the Persian royal court, is said to have asked whether Xerxes wanted a pleasant answer or a truthful one. On being asked to speak the truth he said that the Spartans would never submit to Xerxes, even if all the other Greeks were conquered, because their sense of freedom, duty and obedience allowed them to accept no master but their own laws, which had proven too strong even for Demaratos himself. On the second occasion, at Thermopylai, Demaratos' insistence that the Spartans were the bravest and most independent of the Greeks, and therefore the ones whom Xerxes must do his utmost to defeat, was greeted with scepticism. After the heroic defeat of Leonidas and his Spartan bodyguard, Xerxes changed his mind and asked Demaratos to advise how best to defeat the Spartans. The answer was to use his fleet to bypass the Isthmus of Corinth and to attack Sparta from the sea. His advice was supposedly rejected, although it may well be that it was with this strategy in mind that Xerxes sought to destroy the Greek fleet at Salamis, so that they could not contest any Persian landings on the Peloponnesian coast.

Demaratos never got the chance to return to Sparta as Xerxes' puppet ruler. He must have returned to Persia with Xerxes and lived out his life in exile at the Persian court. His descendants became minor aristocrats in the Persian-controlled territory around the Hellespont, where the Athenian historian Xenophon encountered them early in the fourth century.

Ironically Kleomenes was also deposed as king, because the Spartans discovered the deception that he had practised involving the Delphic oracle, and so he was forced to leave Sparta soon after Demaratos. He tried to get the Arkadians, Sparta's northern neighbours, to help him recover his position and the Spartans reluctantly allowed him to return. Almost immediately, however, he began to behave so violently that his family decided that he had gone mad and had to restrain him. He died almost immediately, but it is unclear whether he committed suicide or was killed by his family. His younger brother Leonidas succeeded him as king.

Demaratos' conversations with Xerxes must be treated with caution, as it is hard to see how Herodotus could have got such detailed information, but the basic story of his exile to Persia and the disappointment of his attempted return can be taken as historically reliable. He had the reputation of being a blunt, but likeable, man. He is once said to have replied in a council meeting to someone who asked him if he was keeping silent because he was stupid, or just at a loss for words, 'Certainly a stupid person would not know when to keep quiet.'

The Greeks attack the Persian Empire

The double victories of Plataia and Mykale were not the end of the Greek and Persian Wars. The Athenians had nurtured ambitions of controlling the Hellespont for several decades. They were increasingly involved in trade with the cities and tribes of the northern Aegean and Black Sea regions. This commercial interest partly explains why Xanthippos and his ships stayed behind in the Hellespont to capture Sestos. The following year, 478, Pausanias took command of the Hellenic League's naval forces and led them on two expeditions, firstly to Cyprus, where the Persians were driven out, and then to Byzantion, which also lost its Persian garrison. Pausanias had his own ambitions, however, and his autocratic style of command and extravagant behaviour now began to upset his allies. The Spartan ephors tried to rein him in but after a return to Sparta for a warning he attempted to set himself up as a tyrant in Byzantion. He was prevented from doing so by an Athenian force under the command of Kimon, the son of Miltiades. He returned to Sparta but quarrelled with the ephors again and had to take refuge in a temple. To avoid offending the gods the Spartans did not try to remove him, preferring to let him starve to death.

Disillusioned with Spartan leadership the Ionian Greeks now turned to Athens. A meeting was held on the island of Delos in 478/77 at which a new alliance was formed. Its members swore to continue the fight against the Persians and to ravage the king's territory in compensation for their own losses. They agreed to put themselves under Athenian leadership and to contribute warships or money to a league fund, administered by Athenian officials called *Hellenotamiai*, meaning 'treasurers of the Greeks'. The numbers of ships or amounts of tribute each island or city was to contribute

were worked out by Aristeides, who was the principal architect of the new alliance. It is known to historians as the Delian League because its treasury was established on Delos.

Themistokles had little to do with the new league, but he did persuade the Athenians to improve the fortifications of their own city and its main port, Peiraieus. The Spartans tried to prevent this development, but Themistokles forestalled their intervention and the Athenians began to turn their city into the strongest in Greece. Eventually they surrounded the whole city and its harbours and the narrow strip of land in between with a set of fortification walls. Themistokles fell out of favour again and in the mid-470s he suffered the indignity of being ostracised by the Athenian assembly. After living in Argos for a short while he went to the Persian court. The Persian king made him a local governor of Magnesia and he died there in 459.

The first major campaign of the Delian League, led by Miltiades' son, Kimon, was against Eion, the final Persian stronghold on the northern coastline of the Aegean. The town was captured in 476. The following year Kimon led the League's forces against a different objective, the island of Skyros, north-east of Euboia. The official reason for conquering this island was that its inhabitants had been practising piracy against merchants sailing through the area, but this seems to have been just the excuse to disguise an act of Athenian imperialism. Kimon 'discovered' a huge human skeleton on the island, claimed it was the bones of the Athenian hero Theseus and returned them to Athens in triumph. Soon afterwards Skyros was settled by Athenians. Another place that felt the growing power of Athens was Karystos on Euboia, which had refused to join the Delian League but was compelled

to do so by another Athenian-led military expedition. When Naxos tried to leave the League in 470 she was attacked, forced to surrender her ships and dismantle her walls and made to pay a monetary tribute. The Delian League was becoming more and more like an Athenian Empire, modelled on the Persian one. That is not to say, however, that the Athenians neglected the aim of making war on the Persian king's territory. In 466 Kimon commanded a large fleet of Delian League ships in a campaign along the south-western coast of Asia Minor to drive the Persians out of the region. It culminated in a battle at the river Eurymedon in Pamphylia at which the Great King's Phoenician fleet of 200 ships was destroyed. Xerxes died in 465 and his son Artaxerxes I failed recover the territory lost to the Delian League. Another major revolt in Egypt between 459 and 454 was aided by an Athenian fleet, but the Persians eventually overcame them and regained control. Soon

This relief sculpture depicting hoplites and a chariot in a formal procession was originally part of the base of a statue. It was probably set up around 490. In 478 the statue base was dismantled and, along with many other pieces of sculpture, it was incorporated into the walls of Athens. The Athenians were in a hurry to complete the walls before the Spartans could interfere and prevent them doing so, and they did not have time to cut and prepare new stones for all of them. (Ancient Art and Architecture)

afterwards Kimon was killed fighting against the Persians in Cyprus and in 449 a peace treaty known as the Peace of Kallias was negotiated between Athens and the Persian king, bringing a halt to their conflicts. By the terms of this treaty the autonomy of the Ionian Greeks was guaranteed, the Persian king agreed that his ships would not sail westwards beyond the Gelidonya islands and that his satraps in Asia Minor would not allow their soldiers to come within a day's ride of the Greeks cities on the coast. In return the Athenians agreed not to make war against the king's territory.

The Peloponnesian War

The Peloponnesian War

The 440s and 430s were a period of great prosperity and power for Athens. The treasury of the Delian League was transferred to the Athenian Acropolis in 454 and detailed records were kept of a tithe of one-sixtieth of the tribute contributions from the allies which was paid to the goddess Athena. From these lists and other sources historians have traced the gradual encroachment of Athens on the autonomy of her League allies, whom they came to regard as subjects of the Athenian Empire. Athens grew richer and spent much of her wealth on magnificent temples and other building projects. The leading Athenian politician of this period was Perikles, the son of Xanthippos, who famously claimed that Athens was providing a lesson to the rest of the Greeks through the excellence of her citizens and scale of their achievements.

The growth of Athenian power caused resentment and fear among many of the other Greek states. The Ionians found that they had exchanged Persian rule for Athenian, and the Spartans, Corinthians and Boiotians became alarmed at Athenian attempts to extend their empire in the Aegean, the western Mediterranean and even on the Greek mainland. After a series of inconclusive conflicts the Spartans were persuaded to lead a coalition of Greek allies in a war against the Athenians. This conflict engulfed most of the Greek world from 431 to 404. It has been called by historians the Peloponnesian War, because most of Sparta's allies were from the Peloponnese. In 413 the Athenians supported a revolt in Karia against the Persian king, Dareios II. This brought the Persians into the Peloponnesian War on the side of the Spartans and their allies. In return for financial and military support against

Athens the Spartans agreed to recognise the Persian king's claim to rule the cities and islands of the Ionian Greeks. The course of the war, which ended in defeat for Athens, is described in Essential Histories (27): *The Peloponnesian War 431–404 BC*.

The King's Peace

The victorious Spartans decided to help themselves to much of what had been the

Athenian Empire. This drew them into further conflict with Persia. In 405/04 Dareios II died and was succeeded by his eldest son Artaxerxes II, but a younger son, Kyros, who had been in charge of helping the Spartans in the Peloponnesian War, resented this and prepared a military expedition to challenge his brother. He asked for Spartan support and was provided with assistance to recruit a force of 10,000 Greek mercenaries, mostly Peloponnesians under the leadership of Spartan officers. He marched his army into Babylonia in 401 and faced his brother's forces in a battle at Kounaxa. Despite the effectiveness of his Greek soldiers Kyros was killed and the 10,000 Greeks had to fight their way out of the Persian Empire to the Hellespont. Their journey was recounted by one of the

participants, Xenophon, an Athenian historian, in a work he called the *Anabasis*, meaning 'the march up country'.

War between Sparta and Persia followed, with the Spartan king, Agesilaos, taking up the cause of freedom for the Greeks in an expedition against the western satrapies of Asia Minor in 396. In response, the Persian king supported other Greek states in a war

This relief sculpture from the Treasury section of the Achaemenid royal place at Persepolis was originally placed in the centre of the ceremonial staircase leading to the magnificent *Apadana* or audience hall. It shows an aristocrat in Median dress paying ritual homage to the king, probably Dareios. In front of the king are two incense-burners. Behind the throne stand his son, Xerxes, a eunuch attendant (he has no beard) and soldiers of the élite regiment of the King's Spearcarriers, who were all members of the Persian aristocracy. (Ancient Art and Architecture)

against Sparta. Ironically the principal Greek ally of the Persians was now Athens. The Athenian general, Konon, was put in charge of the Persian fleet that destroyed the Spartan navy in 394 and removed many Spartan garrisons from the Ionian cities and islands. Konon even used the fleet to help rebuild the fortifications of Athens, which had been destroyed at the end of the Peloponnesian War. The Athenians began to rediscover their own imperial ambitions, however, and in 387/86 a Spartan envoy called Antalkidas was able to negotiate a treaty with the Persian king. Under the terms of this treaty, known as the King's Peace, a general truce was agreed between all the Greek states, with limited autonomy for the Ionian Greeks. Peaceful relations between the Greeks were thus guaranteed by the power of the Persian king. Ultimately the rivalry between the Greeks and the Persians was settled by conquest. Alexander the Great invaded the Persian Empire in 334 and in 330 the last of the Achaemenid kings, Dareios III, was dead and Alexander was the new ruler of an empire that, for a brief period, was even larger than that of Dareios and Xerxes. These events are described in Essential Histories (26): *The Wars of Alexander the Great.*

Further reading

Primary sources

Dillon, M. and Garland, L., *Ancient Greece: Social and Historical Documents from Archaic Times to the Death of Socrates*, London, 1994.

Herodotus, *The Histories*, translated by George Rawlinson, Introduction by Hugh Bowden, Everyman's Library, London, 1992.

The Persian Empire from Cyrus II to Artaxerxes I, translated and edited by Maria Brosius, London Association of Classical Teachers – Original Records Series LACTOR 16, 2000.

Plutarch, *The Rise and Fall of Athens: Nine Greek Lives*, translated by Ian Scott-Kilvert, London, 1960.

Secondary works

Boardman, J., Hammond, N., Lewis, D., Ostwald, M. (editors), *The Cambridge Ancient History Volume 4: Persia, Greece and the Western Mediterranean c. 525 to 479 BC*, 2nd edition, Cambridge, 1988.

Burn, A. R., *Persia and the Greeks. The Defence of the West c. 546–478 BC*, London, 1962; new edition with afterword by David Lewis, 1984.

Cartledge, P., *Spartan Reflections*, London, 2000.

Green, P., *The Year of Salamis 480–479 BC*, London, 1970; revised edition entitled, *The Greco-Persian Wars*, Berkeley and Los Angeles, 1996.

Hanson, V. D., *The Wars of the Ancient Greeks*, London, 1999.

Kuhrt, A., *The Ancient Near East c. 3000–330 BC, Volume Two*, London 1995.

Lazenby, J., *The Spartan Army*, Warminster, 1985.

Lazenby, J., *The Defence of Greece 490–479 BC*, Warminster, 1993.

Sekunda, Nicholas and McBride, A., *The Ancient Greeks*, Oxford, 1986.

Sekunda, N. and Chew, S., *The Persian Army 560–330 BC*, Oxford, 1992.

Index